ONE PEOPLE
ONE PLANET

Advance Praise

"Brilliant writing. Brilliant insight. Brilliant storytelling. At a time when humanity pays a dear and daily price in myriad ways for our loss of a moral consensus, Michael Glauser kindly reminds us of our shared ethical heritage. This book is not just a guide for the perplexed, it is a reliable path to human flourishing."

Joseph Grenny, Co-author of *Crucial Conversations*
Co-founder and Chairman of The Other Side Academy

"How great the need in our world for greater civility! It cannot be legislated. It cannot be mandated. It cannot be enforced. It comes only as individuals internalize principles that produce character and skills imbued with civility. Michael Glauser gives us a proven path to greater happiness and relationships that really works."

Boyd Craig, Founder and CEO of Leader.org
Stephen R. Covey Endowed Professor of Leadership
Huntsman School of Business, Utah State University

"What a compelling read about how to reclaim peace in a world where peace sometimes feels hard to find. It brings the point home beautifully that when we serve, we love; and when we heal our hearts, we can heal the world. Its message is so perfect for our times. Just the salve I needed."

Tessa White, Social Influencer
Founder and CEO of The Job Doctor

"*Elegantly merging ancient time-honored principles with modern science, Mike has crafted a simple but powerful six-step path to greater joy and fulfillment. In a world struggling under the burdens of strife and incivility, this book offers real solutions for personal transformation and social healing.* One People One Planet *is a must-read for everyone interested in bringing about real, positive change in their lives and relationships and the world around them.*"

Chris Dunn
CEO of Mentors International

"*What a beautiful and vital book. Not a day passes when we don't seek the peace of our souls. All of us long for love and the serenity of a settled heart. It goes on deep within us in the midst of conflict and sickness and loss and fearful circumstance. We all live two lives in tandem—what we see and touch, and what is in the shade of our spirits—as vividly real inside as on the outside. We need a new honesty about our material world: it is not enough. We can be One People One Planet when we own the immense invaluable reality that our spiritual 'us' is our first duty. Let life thrive from within.*"

Lord Dr. Michael Hastings of Scarisbrick CBE
House of Lords, Westminster, London
Former Global Head of Citizenship at KPMG

ONE PEOPLE ONE PLANET

6 Universal Truths
for Being Happy Together

MICHAEL GLAUSER

LIONCREST

PUBLISHING

One People One Planet

6 Universal Truths for Being Happy Together

ISBN 978-1-5445-3169-4 Hardcover

978-1-5445-3170-0 Paperback

978-1-5445-3171-7 Ebook

CONTENTS

INTRODUCTION

Our Quest for Happiness

I believe our life on earth can be a beautiful experience, but I am well aware of the challenges it brings. Along with the beauty and joy we often feel, we all experience heartache, loneliness, discouragement, failure, and troubled relationships. These experiences can be very painful and difficult to overcome. In addition, recurring problems seem to cycle through every generation in nearly every country: intolerance, racial discrimination, civil unrest, hatred among political parties, and conflict between nations. It doesn't seem like we learn from our history. But what if we had a credible solution that actually worked to help us overcome the human hardships we face on earth?

I am excited to share a path with you that can help all of us increase our joy and live peacefully together on this planet—and it works for everyone. I have seen it work for convicted felons who have transformed their lives from dark despair to genuine happiness and harmony. I have seen it work for women who have been rescued from the slave trade and are now living lives they never dreamed possible. I have seen it work for people living in poverty around the world who have improved their lives and their communities. Most of all, I have seen it work for everyday men and women who simply want to be happier, healthier, and live more rewarding lives.

This path consists of six enduring principles that have been around for thousands of years. These principles were first introduced and taught by some of the most influential leaders the world has ever known: the Hindu sages discovered them more than 4,000 years ago; Buddha reinforced them 2,500 years ago; Jesus taught them 2,000 years ago; and Muhammad reintroduced them 1,500 years ago. In addition, many philosophers from different countries in different centuries have taught similar principles: Confucius, Plato, Aristotle, Cicero, Aquinas, and Locke. In our own time, recent research in the field of positive psychology has shown that these principles actually do improve the quality of our lives.

These three sources of knowledge—our great religious founders, renowned philosophers, and modern science—have given us a common path we can all follow in life. It doesn't matter who we are, where we live, how we were raised, what we believe, or how much education we have obtained. Following these six principles can help all of us experience greater personal joy, more satisfying relationships, and healthier communities. This shared path can unite us rather than divide us, which is pretty exciting to me.

In the chapters that follow, you will learn more about the common life principles of our greatest teachers and the fascinating research that validates their teachings. You will see how merging ancient wisdom with modern science has produced a path to happiness and civility that works for everyone. You will also hear the stories of remarkable individuals I know who have applied these principles to transform their lives from lingering sorrow to genuine joy. Perhaps most helpful, you will discover tools you can apply to nurture the attributes and assimilate them into your life. Before introducing the six principles, let me briefly tell you how I learned about these universal truths and introduce you to the great teachers who have given them to us.

MY PATH OF DISCOVERY

"You can't talk about politics and you can't talk about religion. If you do, it is grounds for termination. How do you feel about that?"

I was sitting in an office in Houston, Texas, talking with a senior official from the King Fahd University of Petroleum and Minerals (KFUPM), which is located in Dhahran, Saudi Arabia. He was interviewing me for a two-year visiting position in the business school at the university. KFUPM is a premier institution in the Middle East for science, engineering, and business. As a young professor, I was interested in the developing region and the natural resources industry.

"I will be a guest in your country, so I can live with that," I responded.

A few months later, I was sitting in my office in Dhahran talking with one of my new Saudi colleagues. He started asking me questions about my religious background and beliefs.

"I'm sorry, but I can't talk about religion," I replied.

"No, that is not true. You cannot talk about **your** religion, but we can talk to you about **ours**. How much do you know about Islam?" I told him I knew a little bit about his faith and that I would enjoy learning more. He arranged for me to meet with a friend of his who was a religious leader in the community. His friend, Muhammad, was a bright and delightful individual. He agreed to tutor me in Arabic, and I agreed to study Islam with him. We took a trip to the university bookstore, and I came back with an armful of literature on Islam: the Qur'an in both Arabic and English, The Life of the Prophet Muhammad, The Family Structure in Islam, and others. For the next two years, I had a fascinating experience learning about the second-largest religion in the world. I concluded that the original teachings of Islam and Christianity (the religion I was most familiar with) are more alike than they are different.

From that early experience, I became a serious student of world religions and a seeker of truth, wherever I could find it. I have now studied the doctrines and history of Christianity for more than thirty years. I have studied the Holy Qur'an and the hadith of the Prophet, which are the well-documented sayings and actions of Muhammad. I have done in-depth research on the multivolume

Vedas of Hinduism including the Mahabharata, which contains the renowned Bhagavad Gita. And I have read and studied the teachings of Buddha from the Pali canon, the most original and complete compilation of the doctrines of Buddhism.

More than 75 percent of the world's population is affiliated with and influenced by these four major world religions: Christianity (2.4 billion), Islam (1.9 billion), Hinduism (1.2 billion), and Buddhism (500–600 million). Another billion people are affiliated with hundreds of smaller religions, many of which have been influenced by these four. This represents approximately 90 percent of the world's total population. Throughout our lengthy history, we have never had a group of leaders who have had such a major impact on the world; millions of people have been influenced by their teachings in every millennium.

Obvious differences exist among these four major faiths on things we might consider mystical or supernatural—premortal life, the nature of God, life after death, and others. However, if we study the original texts and mark all the verses about how we should live and treat each other on earth, their teachings are nearly identical. This is where we find the six principles for increasing our happiness, improving our relationships, and strengthening our communities.

In addition to studying these four major faiths, I have examined the writings of renowned philosophers as a second source of enlightenment on human happiness. The word *philosopher* comes from a Greek word that means "lover of wisdom." Throughout history, thousands of philosophers have written millions of pages about our human experience. I have focused on a handful that promote key virtues and morals for living a happy and fulfilling life.

Of particular interest is the field of perennial philosophy, developed by Italian scholars during the European Renaissance. Perennial philosophy purports that a single source of knowledge enlightens the world with universal truths about the human condition. Perennial wisdom is therefore timeless and continues to reappear in various civilizations on earth.

In more recent times, the philosopher Aldous Huxley popularized the concept of a single source of enlightenment in his 1945 publication *The Perennial Philosophy*. Huxley argues that we can discover universal realities to transform our mere human condition into a much higher state of happiness. This single source of knowledge—whether it be God, a supreme entity, or an energy field—provides consistent responses to those who seek to improve their lives. Hence, if we seriously search for ways to find lasting joy and live peacefully together on earth, we should all get the same answers. It makes sense that Muhammad, Jesus, Buddha, the Hindu sages, and many philosophers have taught similar principles for human happiness.

Another reason for these common teachings is that we as humans all face the same questions throughout history: What is the purpose of life? What does it mean to live well? How do we become truly happy? Yet, it has only been a few decades since scholars began studying happiness as a legitimate scientific discipline. For many years, the primary focus was on understanding mental disorders and how to cure them. In addition, researchers were not interested in studying religious concepts they believed to be spiritual and mysterious. More recently, the growing field of positive psychology is examining how we can all become happier, healthier, and live more fulfilling lives. As a result, hundreds of studies have been conducted on the same six principles introduced by our religious founders and philosophers. The outcome of this research is clear: these ancient principles really do make our lives better.

THE GREAT TEACHERS

Here is a brief introduction to the great religious founders and philosophers who have given us the six principles for joyful living. This quick review will help you better understand who they were, where they lived, how they discovered their insights, and how influential they have been in our history.

The Hindu Sages

Nearly 5,000 years ago, a multitude of sages in India began exploring the purpose of life and the nature of human consciousness. Their quest was to find a set of changeless principles that would remain constant in our ever-changing world. This process of inquiry was called Brahmavidya, or the "supreme science," and was intended to discover a true and infinite reality that underlies our external world.

The fundamental question asked by these sages was, "Does anything remain the same in the vast array of human experience?" Their exploration led to an immense body of teachings that were passed down orally for many generations. Somewhere between 1,500 and 500 BCE, the teachings of these anonymous sages were written and organized into four works called the Vedas, meaning "knowledge" or "wisdom" in Sanskrit.

An additional volume of Hindu teachings, the Mahabharata, is important to mention. It is a vast epic of history and moral law that was compiled between 500 BCE and 100 CE. Within the Mahabharata is the popular Bhagavad Gita or "Song of the Lord." It tells the story of Prince Arjuna who is going to battle against a branch of his own royal family, which meant many of his friends and relatives would be killed. The Bhagavad Gita is a dialogue between Arjuna and his enlightened charioteer, Krishna, who is an incarnation or avatar of God.

The Bhagavad Gita has been translated into every major language around the world and contains the loftiest Hindu teachings; some compare it to the Sermon on the Mount in Christianity. It is a guide for moral conduct that has influenced many renowned world leaders such as Mahatma Gandhi, Henry David Thoreau, Carl Jung, Ralph Waldo Emerson, and Aldous Huxley.

Buddha

As the Hindu teachings were being compiled, Buddha arrived on the world scene. He was born as Siddhartha Gautama to a royal family in northern India between the sixth and fifth centuries BCE. As a prince in a noble household, Siddhartha's father expected him to become a great king and kept him secluded in the palace where he only saw the luxuries and pleasures of life.

At the age of twenty-nine, Siddhartha became restless and left the safety of his home for the first time. Buddhist tradition teaches that he had four significant encounters known as the four sights, which significantly changed his life. First, he saw an old man who showed him the challenges of aging. Second, he saw a sick man who showed him the disease and pain in the world. Third, he saw a corpse which revealed the final state for all of us. Fourth, he saw an ascetic who was looking for answers to human sorrow.

Siddhartha spent the next six years searching for ways to eliminate human suffering. He tried meditation, fasting, and other methods for achieving enlightenment, but nothing satisfied his quest for truth. Finally, at the age of thirty-five, he sat down under a fig tree and determined not to leave until he understood the true meaning of life. According to Buddhist texts, he sat there for forty-nine days until he received the enlightenment he so desperately sought. The tree became known as the "bodhi" tree or "tree of awakening," and Siddhartha became the Buddha.

Initially, Buddha was reluctant to share his newfound knowledge but realized it was his responsibility to do so. He spent the next forty-five years until his death teaching his principles for eliminating suffering and increasing human happiness. His words were memorized and transmitted orally for nearly five centuries before they were written down by Sri Lankan monks in the Pali language. The Pali canon is believed to be the oldest set of texts that represent the actual words of Buddha.

Jesus Christ

Jesus was the next great teacher to present a plan for peace and happiness to the world. He was born nearly 500 years after the death of Buddha in the first century CE. He was raised as a Jew during the Roman occupation of Israel and became a carpenter like his father, Joseph.

When Jesus was thirty years old, he went into the desert to fast for forty days to gain enlightenment. Following his fast, he was tempted by the adversary prior to beginning his ministry. He was encouraged to turn stones into bread to satisfy his hunger; he was offered the great kingdoms of the world as his own; and he was told to jump from the pinnacle of the temple and ask God to save him. These three temptations symbolize major obstacles to human happiness: the lusts of the flesh, the love of material possessions, and the pride of self-importance. Jesus resisted all three temptations and began his ministry.

The most famous sermon Jesus gave was the Sermon on the Mount, which summarizes his teachings, much like the Bhagavad Gita summarizes Hinduism. This sermon includes numerous topics on moral conduct, including humility, doing good, caring for the needy, not judging others, and forgiveness. Jesus simplified his gospel with two great commandments—to love God and to love our neighbors as ourselves—which he believed encompassed all of the teachings of all the great prophets.

Jesus was tried and crucified for blasphemy and treason just three years after beginning his ministry. His teachings were communicated orally for several decades and then written by various authors forty to eighty years following his death. The twenty-seven books that comprise the New Testament today were organized into one volume sometime during the fifth century, when the various churches at the time finally agreed on what should be included in the Christian canon.

Muhammad

Muhammad appeared on the earth 500 years after Jesus. He was born in Mecca in 570 CE. His father died before his birth, and his mother died when he was six years old. He was raised by his grandfather for two years and then by his uncle. During these early years, Muhammad accompanied his uncle on trade caravans and eventually led caravans throughout the region.

During Muhammad's trading days, there was no central government in the region, and there was frequent fighting among the various family tribes. Many people practiced idolatry and were cruel to the weaker classes, including women and children. Muhammad was a very pensive and compassionate individual and would often retire to a cave outside of Mecca to reflect on these current conditions. In 610 CE, when he was forty years old, the Angel Gabriel appeared to him and told him to "read in the name of the Lord."

Muhammad continued to receive revelations from Gabriel during his life and taught what he learned throughout the region. His mission was to restore the original teachings of the former prophets, which had been altered, lost, or tainted over the centuries. His teachings included the stories of numerous biblical prophets including Adam, Noah, Abraham, Jacob, Joseph, Moses, David, Solomon, and Jesus—who he believed was one of the greatest prophets of all.

Since Muhammad was illiterate, his followers would memorize his words and write them down. It is believed that twenty-nine different scribes recorded his teachings. Muhammad continued to teach the revelations he was receiving for more than twenty years until his death in 632 CE. The following year, his successor, Abu

Bakr, ordered that all the uncollated writings be organized into a single volume: the Qur'an, which means "the recitation" in Arabic. Although the Qur'an is the supreme authority in Islam, the hadith of the Prophet are also part of the Islamic canon of scripture. The hadith, which means "news" or "story," are well-documented sayings of Muhammad that were retold by his followers.

The Philosophers

The teachings of philosophers throughout the ages have been vast and varied. However, when we focus on what they taught about happiness and peaceful living, we find many similarities, which supports the notion of perennial wisdom. Here are a few of the most influential thinkers who have had an impact on the world.

Confucius lived in China around the time of Buddha and is considered the epitome of Chinese sages. He emphasized compassion, humility, forgiveness, generosity, positive relations, and kindness to all. He was the first to introduce a version of the golden rule, "What you do not wish for yourself, do not do to others." The teachings of Confucius have influenced billions of people and become part of the fabric of life in China, Asia, and other parts of the world.

The great Greek philosophers lived between the time of Buddha and Christ, the big three being Socrates, Plato, and Aristotle. Socrates didn't record his teachings, but we learn about them through Plato, his most-prized student. Plato was the founder of the first institute of higher learning in the Western world, and he authored hundreds of manuscripts, 250 of which have survived for more than 2,400 years. Aristotle was one of Plato's students and is considered one of the most influential philosophers of all time. His teachings were accepted by early Christian and Islamic scholars and had a major impact on European philosophers of later centuries. A major emphasis of all three of these Greek philosophers was eudaimonia, which is generally translated as happiness, well-being, and flourishing in life.

The Roman philosophers Cicero and Seneca lived closer to the time of Christ. Cicero wrote extensively but is best known for his book *On Duties*, which he wrote to his son just before he died. This book summarizes his preeminent principles on how to live—similar to the Bhagavad Gita and the Sermon on the Mount. Approximately 700 original handwritten copies of this work still exist today, and it was the third book ever printed on the Gutenberg press (the first being the Gutenberg Bible). Seneca followed Cicero and championed what is known as the Stoic philosophy. He taught that happiness is the ultimate goal of life and that we obtain it by developing our true potential as human beings. Our challenge in life is to close the gap between who we are now and who we are capable of becoming.

The writings of the Greek and Roman philosophers had a huge impact on scholars and philosophers of later centuries. For example, Saint Thomas Aquinas spent his life merging Aristotle's philosophies with Christian doctrines. Marsilio Ficino, a founder of perennial philosophy, translated the writings of Plato from Greek to Latin. And John Locke was heavily influenced by Cicero's writings on equality and human rights. It is interesting to note that Thomas Jefferson borrowed Locke's most lofty concepts when writing the Declaration of Independence—concepts that originated with Cicero.

A PATH TO HAPPINESS AND CIVILITY

The six universal principles introduced by our great teachers provide a strong path to happiness and civility in our lives. Following this path leads to joy, peace, and satisfying relationships. If we veer from this path, we are more likely to experience sorrow, unhappiness, and troubled relationships.

As you learn about the six principles, you will see that happiness and civility are inseparably connected. The principles produce greater happiness and also greater civility in our relationships. Civility cannot be legislated, mandated, or enforced by governments—it comes from internalizing civil values in our lives. In other words, as we become happier, we also become more civil, and becoming more civil reinforces our happiness.

Figure I-1 illustrates the six principles in the path to happiness and civility. Although we will discuss them in more depth in the following chapters, I will briefly review them here so you will understand what they are and how they fit together.

Figure I-1: A Path to Happiness and Civility

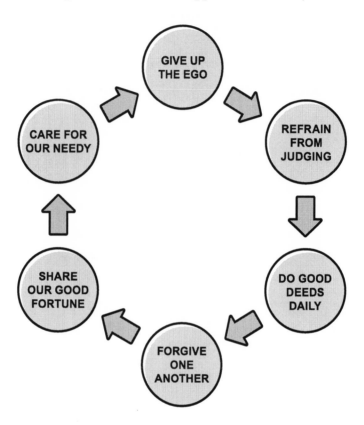

Give Up the Ego

We all possess "two selves" in this life. One is our "true self," which has tremendous potential to learn, grow, and obtain genuine happiness. The second is our "ego," which develops based on our experiences, feedback from others, successes, and failures. In other words, it is a fabrication we carry around with us that isn't who we really are or could become. This "egoic self" sets bounds and limitations on our lives and can highjack our happiness. Giving up this artificial ego opens our lives to greater growth and more authentic joy.

Refrain from Judging

We construct images of other people in the same way we construct images of ourselves. These perceptions are often based on rather superficial cues: color, race, nationality, physical features, education, livelihood, place of residence, and so on. The problem is, our perceptions of others are often inaccurate and sometimes dead wrong. These biases we develop can lead to personal alienation, divisions between groups, and tension in communities. Overcoming our tendencies to judge leads to more satisfying relationships and greater happiness.

Do Good Deeds Daily

As we give up our egos and refrain from judging, we are more inclined to engage in good deeds in our relationships and our communities. Good deeds obviously benefit the receivers of the kindness, but they also benefit the givers. Numerous studies show that serving others can significantly improve our emotional health, physical health, and even our longevity. In addition, doing good deeds helps us realize we have value and something to contribute to the world, which increases our feelings of self-worth and overall life satisfaction.

Forgive One Another

The more relationships we develop in life, the more likely we are to offend and be offended by others. Making mistakes is a normal part of our human experience. Holding grudges against people who harm us, however, can canker our souls—it's like drinking poison and waiting for the other person to die. Forgiving one another is a critical component for healing ourselves emotionally and increasing our personal peace.

Share Our Good Fortune

Craving for possessions can lead to sorrow when we don't have them, but obtaining them creates a different set of problems: attachment, greed, hoarding, lust, and fear of losing what we have. None of our great sages taught that having material possessions, or even great wealth, is wrong. What is wrong is an intense attachment and love for these things. Research confirms that attachment to material possessions can produce stress and frustration, while generosity is related to vitality, self-esteem, and overall quality of life.

Care for Our Needy

We are all connected as a human family and our actions cause ripples of reactions around us. Hence, if we take care of the needy, we are taking care of ourselves and our communities. When we mentor the poor in basic principles of self-reliance, household income goes up, nutrition improves, children are able to go to school, families are happier, and the economy of the community improves. Also remarkable, when the poor start developing modest means, they often become generous givers themselves.

When we strive to apply these six principles in our lives, we find that they build on each other. As we give up our mortally constructed ego, we are less judgmental and more open to others. As we refrain from superficial judgments, we are more inclined to do good deeds for people. As we devote time to serving others, we are more forgiving when offenses occur. As our relationships grow stronger, we are more likely to detach from our possessions and share what we have. As our capacity to share expands, we find those among us who truly need our assistance. If we continue to cycle through this process, the principles become a more permanent part of our lives. Our challenges will not go away, but we will be happier, have greater support in life, and be more resilient when hardships arise.

THE PROMISE

The Hindu sages, Buddha, Jesus, Muhammad, and various philosophers taught what they believed to be true principles. However, they didn't ask people to take their word for it alone. Rather, they asked their followers to practice the principles to see if they worked. In other words, just do it and see what happens.

All of these leaders promise that our lives will start shifting from darker to brighter days as we implement their teachings. In Hinduism and Buddhism, this movement to greater light occurs through the law of karma. The underlying assumption is that everything in our world is connected and in constant motion. Hence, all of our actions eventually produce equal reactions in kind. Harmful deeds yield negative consequences (dark karma), and good deeds yield positive consequences (bright karma). Jesus and Muhammad taught a similar concept of "reaping what we sow." Good deeds bring forth good fruit, while harmful deeds bring forth corrupt fruit.

In addition to karma, Hinduism teaches that greater light comes as we move through three mental states called gunas: (1) Tamas is the lowest level of ignorance, insensitivity, unhappiness, and darkness; (2) Rajas is a state of striving that can be positive or negative depending on our actions; (3) Sattva is the highest level of goodness, harmony, and light. The Hindu promise is, "When sattva predominates, the light of wisdom shines through every gate of the body." This movement from darkness to light is illustrated in Figure I-2.

Figure I-2: The Continuum of Light

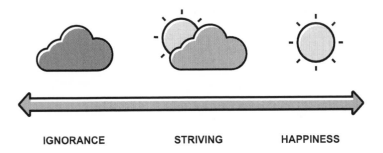

IGNORANCE   STRIVING   HAPPINESS

All of us can obtain greater light in our lives if we follow the path to get us there. I like to compare this higher level of happiness to the brilliance of the sun. The sun is always shining, but we don't always see its light—clouds develop, storms arise, and night falls regularly. But if we board an airplane and fly above the earth's surface, we see that the sun is always shining. All we have to do is raise ourselves to a higher level to experience its power. Likewise, applying the six universal truths will lead us to a higher level of joy and a much brighter countenance.

In conclusion, we live in a world that emphasizes differences between people, groups, races, religions, and nations. This fixation on differences has a purpose. It helps us understand our world, where we fit in, and how to behave around certain groups. However, a constant diet of differences can lead to distrust, separation, conflict, and marginalizing whole groups of people.

We share far more similarities as humans than we do differences. We have common physical attributes, we share 99 percent of the same DNA, and we have similar emotions and aspirations for ourselves and our loved ones. Focusing on similarities does not mean we are naive about differences among us, but it produces far more positive outcomes in our lives: it helps us eliminate our biases, develop deeper friendships, collaborate on challenges, and create stronger unity in our communities.

We are one people on one planet—we are all in this life together. My hope is that we can think more about similarities and how to make our experience on earth better for everyone. As you read the chapters that follow, you will begin creating your own plan for increased joy and harmony. As the process begins to yield fruit, you will become a brighter light to others. As they follow your example, the principles will continue to spread. Eventually, this can impact families, communities, and nations—which is a goal worth pursuing.

Chapter 1

GIVE UP THE EGO

David Durocher was on the run. He had been weighing drugs for sale at a friend's house when he noticed a helicopter hovering in the sky; he thought it was odd that it wasn't going anywhere. When he loaded the drugs in his car and drove away, he was immediately pursued by what "seemed like one hundred cop cars." After already serving four consecutive prison terms, he knew he could not go back, so he became like a NASCAR driver leading the pack on a high-speed chase—racing through stoplights, hitting cars, showing no regard whatsoever for public safety. He was trying to get to a bridge in Huntington Beach, where he could throw the drugs out the window and into the water. Before he got there, he hit a police roadblock and made a quick decision: this would be "suicide by cop." He slammed his car into the roadblock believing they would shoot him. Death was a far better option than spending the rest of his life in a six-by-eight-foot prison cell.

David started getting into trouble when he was six years old. "I was like Dennis the Menace in my younger years." He stole mail from mailboxes, broke into people's homes, and rummaged through their cupboards and refrigerators. His frustrated father started telling him he was no good and tried various forms of punishment to control his behavior. "I was literally on restriction at times for entire summers; I was a prisoner in my room. Mom and Dad had no idea how to deal with me."

When David was twelve years old, he started sneaking his father's alcohol and replacing it with water. At thirteen, he did his first line of cocaine and continued using through high school. During this time, he gravitated to a rougher crowd of friends and became their leader. "I learned that it was much easier to lead among losers than to lose among leaders. I started to feel like I had an identity, and my reputation meant the world to me."

When David graduated from high school, he started using methamphetamine, and that's when the wheels of his life came off completely: addiction, drug dealing, gun running, violence, and assault. His first prison term was two years, and although it was a horrible experience, it didn't change him. He was out for fifty-nine days and then back for five more years. He made it sixty days after this release and then served a six-year term. Next time around, he was a bit smarter but not much; he made it four months before receiving a ten-year sentence for multiple crimes.

David became the prison yard boss during his multiple sentences. He was the leader of the "white guys" and had a reputation as the toughest, meanest, nastiest guy in the place. This reputation was extremely important to him. "I was willing to fight. I was willing to cut somebody. I was willing to stab somebody. I was willing to be on the front line of a riot. I was willing to do all of those things for what I thought was the cause in prison."

David was now on the run again. Unfortunately for him—or so he believed at the time—he was not killed at the roadblock in

Huntington Beach. He was pulled from his car and "beaten senseless" by a group of police officers. The last thing he remembered before passing out was someone yelling, "Stop! You're going to kill him." David woke up in jail facing a twenty-nine-year prison term this time, which was plea-bargained down to twenty-two years. How did his life come to this? What decisions put him on this miserable path? What attitudes and behaviors accelerated his wasted life? He was going to have a lot of time to contemplate these questions.

David Durocher is now the Executive Director of The Other Side Academy in Salt Lake City, one of the most successful life-changing programs in the world for convicted felons, drug addicts, and homeless individuals. He has lived in both heaven and hell, and heaven is far greater than anything he ever imagined. His new dream is to help thousands of people living desperate lives find genuine happiness and learn to live peacefully with others. How in the world did he go from years of crime and incarceration to one of the happiest people on the planet?

* * *

Salsa Queen Zapata is now her legal name. It used to be Maharba Zapata. Maharba is Abraham spelled backward, which was her father's name. Maharba grew up in Mexico with her parents and siblings. Early in life, she decided she wasn't very smart. She did poorly in school because things didn't always make sense to her. Later in life, she found out she has dyslexia and is color-blind which explains her poor performance. She still remembers one embarrassing experience she had as a student.

> Let me tell you what a dummy I was in school. One time I made the mistake of asking, "Are we outside the world, not inside it? Then how do we not fall off?"

When Maharba was a teenager, her father came to America illegally to earn money for the family. They were very poor at the time and often only had beans and tortillas for dinner. A year later, the rest of the family came to America on visitors' visas and never went back. All they brought with them was what would fit in a few suitcases because they couldn't look like they were staying long term.

Maharba's parents got a job cleaning a local grocery store and were allowed to take home food that had expired each day: milk, cheese, bread, meat, and so on. "The cheese was green, so we cut the green off and ate the rest. We were in heaven; we were so thankful."

Maharba went to the local high school to enroll that first year, but she didn't speak English and couldn't complete all the required forms, so she never went back. It wasn't long before she became pregnant and was a single mom. Her new baby was diagnosed with leukemia and spent eighteen months in the hospital, which is where Maharba learned to speak English.

Eventually, the child had a bone marrow transplant—Maharba was the donor—but it didn't take, and the child died. When people told Maharba how sorry they were about her loss, she replied, "It's just part of life"—at least it was part of the way her life had been going. She went on to have seven more children and two divorces.

> Since I didn't finish high school and was a stay-at-home mom, I always believed very strongly that I had no talents. Everybody had talent but me. Why was I born without a talent? I guess my talent was to bear kids, and I was okay with that.

After her second divorce, she became severely depressed. She had no talents, no skills, no way to make a living, and no hope for a better future. At one point, she thought ending her life might be the best solution to her problems, but she continued to struggle to survive.

Today, Maharba is the owner and CEO of Salsa Queen, a highly successful company that makes gourmet salsas. "I always tell people we are the Chanel of salsas." She has dozens of employees, and her products are sold in hundreds of grocery stores around the country —including the one her parents worked in when they came to America. She has an attractive home, is providing for her family, and is happier than she has ever been. When she received her US citizenship, she changed her legal name to Salsa Queen. So how does someone like Maharba with a crippling self-identity go from where she was to where she is now?

THE GREAT TEACHERS
ON EGO

The Hindu Sages

Hinduism teaches that we all have two selves: our false self and our true self. Our false self or "ego" is a composite of our mortal experiences—our interactions with others, our physical qualities, our worldly possessions, and so forth. Our true "self" or "atman" is our inner soul and the essence of our nature—it is eternal, imperishable, and unbounded in potential for growth and happiness. Numerous Hindu texts teach that these two selves exist in everyone.

> Like two golden birds perched on the selfsame tree, intimate friends, the ego and the Self dwell in the same body.
>
> The Self is hidden in the hearts of all, as butter lies hidden in cream.
>
> There are two selves, the separate ego and the indivisible Atman. When one rises above I and Me and Mine, the Atman is revealed as one's real Self.

The false self or ego is seen in Hinduism as an illusion, rather than who we really are or could become. Living life according to the dictates of our ego, rather than seeking our true self, leads to a life of craving, attachment, and sorrow.

As long as we think we are the ego, we feel attached and fall into sorrow.

The ego gropes in darkness, while the Self lives in light.

An important goal in Hinduism is to liberate ourselves from the illusions of our ego and the material world. As we seek to discover our true self, we slowly remove layers of misperceptions the world has imposed on us. This process releases us from our illusionary prison and puts us on the path to ultimate joy and happiness.

Buddha

Buddha also introduced two concepts of the self, similar to Hinduism: the atta and the anatta. The atta is the self or ego that develops and becomes fairly solid over time. It is based on our experiences, interactions, consequences, and attachment to things. According to Buddha, this self or ego is nothing more than a fabricated delusion—it is not who we are or could become in life. Clinging to this delusional self can be a source of great unhappiness. It puts us at the center of everything, limits our personal growth, and hinders our happiness.

In contrast, the anatta is a state of nonself, egolessness, or selflessness. According to Buddha, since the delusional self is only a set of perceptions, there is not a singular entity that we can actually define as the self. If we follow his path for alleviating suffering, we can extinguish our fabricated self and move into a far more rewarding state of nonself. In this state, the self is not the center of everything we do.

Buddha's concept of "impermanence" helps explain the "nonself." He taught that everything in the world is in constant flux; change is not just a part of life but life itself. Our physical world is changing constantly, and so are we as humans. Buddha would agree with Heraclitus, the Greek philosopher who lived at the time of Buddha, who said, "No man ever steps in the same river twice, for it's not the same river and he's not the same man."

If we let our limiting self-perceptions govern our lives, we continue to live as we have been, not as we could. As we transition from a state of self to nonself, we free ourselves from the claustrophobia of self-centeredness. We no longer fret about our past, obsess about ourselves, or worry about our future. It is like awaking from a deep sleep and discovering a much larger world. We become one with other people and enjoy a more authentic and lasting happiness.

Jesus Christ

Jesus taught that we all have an immortal soul or spirit that will live beyond this life. This is our true and eternal self. Our spirit resides within our mortal body here on the earth. Although the body can be a great gift, it is susceptible to lust, selfishness, envy, and strife. An important part of life is learning to harness the mortal self and live according to our spiritual self, which is characterized by love, joy, and peace. Christ taught his followers to "Watch and pray that ye enter not into temptation: the spirit is indeed willing, but the flesh is weak."

An important part of controlling the flesh is to keep our ego or attitude of superiority in check. On numerous occasions, Christ taught his followers to humble themselves and overcome their sense of self-importance.

> For everyone that exalteth himself shall be abased, and he that humbleth himself shall be exalted.
>
> Whosoever will be great among you, let him be your minister. And whosoever will be chief among you let him be your servant.

If we constantly focus on ourselves and our own interests, we live a very narrow and less fulfilling life. When we get outside of ourselves and think more about others, we discover who we really are, our true potential, and what we have to contribute to the world. Perhaps this is what Christ meant when he said, "He that findeth his life shall lose it, but he that loseth his life for my sake shall find it."

Muhammad

The Prophet Muhammad was a humble man who lived a simple life. He regularly ate with the poor, played with the children, made his own clothing, and milked his own sheep. He was very loving, forgiving, and unselfish with his time, teachings, and means. He constantly taught his followers to shed any feelings of pride, superiority, or self-importance.

> Do not strut arrogantly about the earth: you cannot break it open, nor match the mountains in height.

> The servants of the Lord of Mercy are those who walk humbly on the earth, and who, when aggressive people address them, reply, with words of peace.

> Do not turn your nose up at people, nor walk about the place arrogantly...and lower your voice, for the ugliest of all voices is the braying of asses.

Muhammad was also a huge proponent of equal treatment for everyone, regardless of position or status in life. This was an extremely controversial message during a time of widespread slavery, racism, and tribalism. He even asked his followers to free their slaves and make them full partners in their possessions, which many did.

Muhammad delivered his last sermon just prior to his death in 632 CE during his final pilgrimage to Mecca. In this speech, he emphasized the most salient parts of his teachings. It was a remarkable declaration of human rights for the seventh century, including references to racism, women's rights, and income inequality. Of particular interest is his strong conviction that no one is superior to anyone else in life, a message that is still needed today.

An Arab has no superiority over a non-Arab, nor does a non-Arab have any superiority over an Arab; a white has no superiority over a black, nor does a black have any superiority over a white except by piety and good action.

The Philosophers

Many philosophers talked about the dual nature of the self—a lesser self and a loftier self. Most agree that happiness is a function of discovering who we really are and then living in accordance with our true self. Plato, in particular, gave us a wonderful image of a chariot attached to two horses; one is dark and one is light. The dark horse represents our mortal self, our vices, and our unhealthy attitudes. In contrast, the light horse represents our nobler self and what we have the potential to become. In the story, the charioteer is driving the horses into the heavens. The light horse wants to rise up, but the dark horse keeps pulling the chariot back to earth. Plato concludes that letting the dark horse lead is a "ruthless enslavement" of our divine nature. Following the light horse has far more potential to lead us to eudaimonia or full human flourishing.

This analogy provides a great framework for analyzing our self-perceptions. We can regularly ask ourselves this question: Am I listening to the dark horse (my lesser self), which leads to limitations and stagnation, or am I listening to the light horse (my loftier self), which leads to growth and happiness?

THE SCIENCE ON EGO

Sigmund Freud introduced the idea of an ego early in the twentieth century. He claimed there are three parts to our personality: the id, the superego, and the ego. The id is our primitive and impulsive nature that wants immediate pleasure and gratification. The superego is our conscience or moral compass that tells us what is acceptable and unacceptable in society. The ego is our conscious mind that mediates between the id and superego and becomes our identity or concept of self. The word *ego* in Latin actually means "I." Although we tend to think of the ego as a cocky attitude of self-importance, it is actually the way we define ourselves throughout our lives, either positive or negative.

Many scholars and social scientists have expanded the concept of the ego or self-identity since the time of Freud. Most agree our ego starts to develop in early childhood, becomes stronger during adolescence, and is fairly well defined by adulthood. It is shaped by feedback we receive about ourselves from parents, teachers, peers, the media, and our culture. This myriad of messages teaches us who we are, what we are like, where we are strong, where we are weak, how valuable we are, and what we have to contribute. We might compare our mind to a computer and our ego is the sum of all the software and apps about ourself that have been downloaded into our consciousness.

Numerous studies show that our perceived self-identity has a significant impact on our lives. It influences our communication, behavior, relationships, decision making, judgments of others, buying behavior, food choices, and so on. As we act in accordance with our ego, the feedback we receive reinforces our self-identity; hence, our ego becomes a victim of itself and continues to influence our behavior in predictable ways. Although our self-identity can continue to develop throughout our lives, our self-perceptions remain fairly stable in adulthood.

The fact that we all have an ego is not all bad. It helps us control our impulses, gives us a reliable sense of self, and helps us navigate our world. Unfortunately, our ego can also foster a host of undesirable characteristics such as superiority, rigidity, jealousy, defensiveness, anxiety, and hopelessness. Many therapists believe our ego is the major source of our problems and miseries in life, and their therapies are aimed at helping people develop a healthier and more functional self-identity.

Another less desirable thing our ego does is make constant comparisons with other people. Some of us do this more than others, but we all tend to evaluate how we fit into our social environment. It is like we are climbing a ladder and people are either above us or below us in various aspects of our identity. When we move up a rung in our own mind, someone else moves down. It's as though we are the main actor in our own internal movie. Social media has made this process worse, as we post things about our "ideal" lives—relaxing on a beach, skiing in the mountains, welcoming a new baby, hugging loved ones, and so on. Even though these experiences are awesome, they don't represent the full picture of heartaches, challenges, and failures we all experience.

Recent studies show that we feel better about ourselves as we make comparisons to people who are below us on the social ladder. However, when we compare ourselves to people we believe are above us, we tend to ruminate more about ourselves and have more depressing thoughts. This continual process of comparison can lead to two outcomes: a seriously inflated ego that says we are better than other people (David Durocher) or an overly deflated ego that says we are not as good as other people (Salsa Queen). Table 1-1 shows some of the attitudes and behaviors that are associated with these two extremes.

Table 1-1: Two Distorted Egos

SIGNS OF AN INFLATED EGO	SIGNS OF A DEFLATED EGO
Talks about self constantly	Afraid to express views and ideas
Strives to be in the spotlight	Doesn't want to be seen or heard
Knows more than other people	Not as smart as everyone else
Defensive in disagreements	Yields to others in differences
Threatened by people's successes	Everyone else is more successful
Belittles other people regularly	Not as good as other people
Won't admit mistakes or weakness	Blames self for most problems
Takes credit for group successes	Has little to contribute to others

Our egos can cause us to obsess more about ourselves than others. As soon as we get out of bed, we worry about how our day will go, we wonder how others will perceive us, we ruminate about ourselves during conversations, we wonder if we've said the right things, we worry about mistakes we've made, and on and on. It's like being trapped on a claustrophobic treadmill of self-centeredness.

A group of scholars recently developed a method for assessing the strength of the ego on a scale from "noisy" to "quiet." The "noisy ego" is self-centered, defensive, and unaware of the needs and perspectives of others. In contrast, the "quiet ego" is humble, nondefensive, aware of the needs and perspectives of others, and interested in personal development. Numerous studies show that people with a quiet ego

- have greater self-compassion,

- positively manage their emotions,

- experience lower levels of stress,

- are able to persevere in adversity, and

- enjoy greater life satisfaction.

A similar line of research has been occurring in organizations for the past few decades. The concept of "servant leadership" is comparable to the "quiet ego." Servant leaders are other-oriented and focus on the needs, capabilities, and potential of their followers. They don't ignore performance, but the development of their people is their primary focus. Servant leadership can be applied by people in any type of organization: business, nonprofit, government, education, families, and communities.

By contrast, traditional authoritarian leaders have a strong self-interest. They operate from the top of a hierarchy and use their position and power to achieve results that make them look good. They don't hesitate to sacrifice their people to the profits and performance of the organization, which sounds a lot like a "noisy ego." Hundreds of studies have shown that servant leadership, as opposed to autocratic leadership, produces a number of attractive outcomes in organizations:

- Trust in the leader is higher.

- Collaboration is better.

- Job satisfaction is higher.

- Team performance is better.

- Member turnover is lower.

One of the best examples I have seen of a servant leader with a quiet ego is Mel Torrie, founder of Automated Solutions. Mel's company builds robots and unmanned vehicles for the mining, agriculture, military, and construction industries. Mel has more than a hundred well-educated team members working with him—most are engineers, and many have master's degrees and PhDs. They build everything from small bomb-removing robots to massive trucks that operate without a driver.

Mel is a lifetime student of leadership and is always searching for ways to improve his company. He became discouraged when he learned that Steve Jobs was an abrasive and autocratic leader—he was confrontational, controlling, and ruthless when people didn't perform well. Mel knew he needed to push his people in order to become a world-class company, but he was not at all like Steve Jobs and didn't want to be.

After a great deal of study and thought, Mel developed his "Humble" program. The idea is that team members need to check their egos at the door, freely share their ideas, willingly accept feedback, and collaborate to achieve their full, ultimate potential. Mel believes that being humble is the overarching quality that helps us develop our other character traits. He feels it is absolutely essential for achieving the lofty goals he has for his company: to be a place where people want to work even if they don't have to, and to provide financial independence for all team members.

Mel has developed an assessment tool to measure "Humble," which he administers quarterly and talks about constantly with his team members. So how well is his program working? Under Mel's leadership, Automated Solutions has grown to one of the largest privately held robotics solutions companies in the world. Mel believes his "Humble" program has significantly shaped the culture of the company and plays a huge role in their success. He regularly hears comments like, "My leader really listens to me," "I have an impact in the organization," and "I love coming to work every day."

Although humility is one of the hardest qualities to develop, it is a key ingredient for achieving our potential, working cooperatively with others, and enjoying greater satisfaction in our lives and careers. So how do we lose our preconceived ego and cultivate a healthier and more functional self-identity? Let's return to Dave Durocher and Salsa Queen.

THE REST OF THE STORY

David Durocher knew about a program for convicted felons called Delancey Street. It is an alternative to prison for criminals who are ready and capable of change. He applied to the program ten years earlier but was not accepted. He was still too proud, cocky, and full of himself. "I wouldn't have accepted myself either," David recalls.

Now he was facing a twenty-two-year sentence and feared he would die in prison. He was scared, depressed, and broken. He wrote another letter to Delancey Street, and this time he begged the interviewer to give him a chance. He was accepted into the program and the judge reluctantly agreed to let him go, although he was not optimistic that David would succeed.

Delancey Street is a training school that operates a variety of enterprises. Each resident is assigned to work in one of the departments. David wanted to work in construction, ceramics, warehousing, the moving company, or the woodshop. In fact, with his superb gang leadership skills, he thought he should be running the place. The only place he didn't want to work was in landscaping. When he was young, his dad made him mow their lawn with a push mower and weed the entire perimeter of the yard, and he hated it! His first assignment was in landscaping. "I was beside myself. Who do you think you are, calling me to landscaping? I am capable of so much more. All they told me was to shut up and go to work."

Every morning David's supervisor, Jimmy, would let his little dog Baxter poop where David was working. He couldn't believe this was happening to the former prison yard boss who was good enough to be running the facility.

> I got so mad I wanted to drop kick that dog onto the 101 freeway and then smack Jimmy with the shovel. That is how bad I still was. I had just beaten a twenty-two-year prison sentence, yet I was too proud to pick up dog poop with a shovel. It turns out that steaming helping of humility was exactly what I needed. Today, I would pick up that dog poop with my bare hands. Who cares?

David started to feel real gratitude that he was at Delancey Street and not in prison. He decided to focus on other people rather than himself, which was a major mental shift after decades of putting himself first in everything he did. Soon he had the nickname Dinner Date Dave because every morning he would make a request to have dinner with a different person. He thrived on meeting with the newer residents and sharing things he was learning about becoming a decent, honest, accountable human being.

> I started to influence people and make a difference in their lives. It started to feed my soul, and I loved how that made me feel. Pretty soon, I needed more of that. As a drug addict, you always want more and more and more. I just made people my new drug and it became my new high—it's also free and there is no "comedown." Impacting people for good is the best feeling in the world. I took off that black hat and put on the white one, and I have never looked back.

David Durocher has had a positive impact on thousands of lives and is happier than he has ever been. It's all about learning humility, getting over our false selves, and taking the actions required to create a more functional self-identity. David is a firm believer that anyone can do this.

> Even the most broken people can reinvent themselves and become somebody they have never known. It doesn't matter if you have lived your life on the streets, been a lifelong drug addict, or spent your life in and out of jails and prisons. Guys like us change by doing; what that means is "acting as if." Act as if you are honest until you become honest; act as if you are accountable until you become accountable; do the next right thing every single day for hundreds of days until you

have a paradigm shift in the way you think; and that becomes you. Anyone can change.

* * *

Maharba met Jim during her darkest days, just after her second divorce. He asked her, "What would you like to do?" No one had ever asked her that question before. Since she loves food, Jim helped her explore several options for food businesses. She chose salsas because that is part of her heritage—it is what she knows and what she loves.

Maharba started making salsas in her small kitchen with her kids. They created six incredible recipes and started selling them on Facebook. When people ordered her salsas, she would meet them in a parking lot to deliver the products. "We were like salsa dealers in the parking lot, exchanging salsa for money."

Next, she took her salsas to the local farmers' market. A food expert she met told her to take only fifty products—he didn't want her to bring home unsold salsas and be discouraged. She took one hundred products and sold them all in two hours. "I was so excited I had $500 in my hand. It was the most money I had ever earned in my life."

With her growing confidence, she approached several small grocery stores which agreed to carry her products. Then she decided to contact a larger chain—Smith's Food and Drug. When she called their office, the buyer said he wasn't interested in another salsa brand.

But when she told him, "These are fresh salsas made locally by me and my kids," he agreed to meet with her.

Maharba went to the meeting decked out in her Salsa Queen attire: bright colors, Salsa Queen apron, big Mexican flower in her hair. She carried her products into the meeting in a Costco bag. She had no idea that Smith's Food and Drug was owned by Kroger, the largest supermarket chain in the country.

The buyer took a few minutes to taste her salsas and said, "You're in." He then invited fifteen more people into the room to taste her products. Maharba was confused and didn't know what was happening. After a while, the buyer told her she needed to meet with his administrator to get things started. Before he left, he said, "You are going to have to hire more than your kids." The administrator set up the account and gave her some important advice.

> Maharba, in the seventeen years that I have been here, this has never happened. People die to be in your spot, so take care of your spot and take care of your product.

Maharba hired a few people and met all of her orders. "I was not going to fail them." This was her biggest success to date. She now employs dozens of people, has a large manufacturing facility, and sells her products to hundreds of grocery stores across the country. She gives her friend Jim a great deal of the credit for her success. "He was the first person to really believe in me." Jim eventually quit his job at the bank, started working at Salsa Queen full time, and married Maharba.

In addition to Jim's influence, each small step Maharba took gave her the confidence to take another bigger step: from Facebook to the farmers' market, to several small grocery stores, to a national chain, to a large production facility, to thousands of delighted customers across the country. This process has totally changed her limiting self-identity. She has shed her old ego, realized her potential, created a much healthier self—including her new name, Salsa Queen—and is happier than she has ever been.

> Never in my honest dreams did I think I would be where I am. I started Salsa Queen to provide for myself and my kids, and now I am providing for many more people and still growing. I feel confident. I feel like I have a voice. I feel strong and powerful. I see myself as beautiful now.

THE APPLICATIONS

1. Know That You Are Not Your Ego

The first step in losing our constructed ego is to realize what it is —it is not who we really are but who we perceive ourselves to be. It develops during our early years from numerous messages we receive about ourselves—some of these are fact and some of them are fiction. Our ego then functions to preserve itself in our later years; it's like a voice telling us a story about who we are over and over again. Some of us develop inflated egos and some of us develop deflated egos. Most of us end up with a mixed bundle of both positive and negative self-perceptions. Realizing there are whole new possibilities for ourselves is a key to change.

Some psychologists suggest we give our ego a different name to remind us it is our perceived self-talking, not our potential self. For example, if you ruminate on a negative perception of yourself, you might say, "That's Mikey talking, not Michael." Or if you doubt you can accomplish something based on your past experiences, you might say, "That's little Sarah talking, not me." This will help remind us that our ego is a separate entity from who we really are or can become. Learning to challenge our fictional self puts us on a path to greater happiness and better relationships.

2. Examine Your Habitual Self-Perceptions

To help pay my tuition as a college student, I started teaching piano lessons at a local music store. I noticed that many of my young students had preconceived notions of how well they would do before they even started their lessons. I would hear things like, "My sister is really good at music, but I'm not." Or "I am really good at sports but not very good at the piano." When I asked them where these perceptions came from, they would mention one or more experiences they had with parents, teachers, siblings, or peers: "You are really tone-deaf"; "It drives me crazy when you bang on that piano."

I tried to counteract these early perceptions by telling my students that anyone can learn to play the piano if they really want to and are willing to practice hard. I continued to reinforce this message as my students made progress. Although some did better than others, it was fun to see many of them overcome their original assessment of their ability and become talented piano players. Developing this skill seemed to make a difference in their lives.

Understanding where our self-perceptions have come from is an important step in altering them. Socrates was a huge proponent of self-examination as a way to gain greater wisdom about ourselves and our lives. He made his famous statement, "The unexamined life is not worth living" while he was on trial for corrupting the youth. He believed that examining who we are, what drives us, and why we respond the way we do is critical to our growth and happiness in life. If we get up and do the same things over and over again every day without much self-reflection, we are not adding value to our own lives or to others.

As humans, we are quick to attribute thoughts and motives to others —even though we are usually wrong—but not as likely to examine our own self-identity. Here is a process for self-reflection that can help: Sit in a comfortable chair for ten minutes each day and select one of your personal attributes to examine. For example, do you feel superior or inferior to others? Are you attractive or unattractive? Are you friendly or unfriendly? Are you intelligent or challenged? Are you positive or pessimistic? Are you creative or unimaginative?

Are you athletic or uncoordinated? Now ask yourself these questions:

- How do I describe myself on this quality?

- When were my first thoughts that I am this way?

- What messages did I receive about this quality?

- What are the positive outcomes of this perception?

- What are the negative outcomes of this perception?

- How would I like to be in the future on this quality?

- How would I think if I had this new perception?

- How would I act if I had this new perception?

Understanding how our ego has evolved is an important step in dislodging our old identity and developing a healthier sense of self. The next essential step is to take action.

3. Stretch to Actions beyond Your Ego

At the end of my bachelor's degree, I needed one more class to graduate. I had a job at the time and needed a course that would fit my schedule. The only class offered when I was available was a graduate-level seminar. I approached the professor who said, "This class is for master's and PhD students, so you would have a really hard time." The class was clearly outside my confidence zone, but I convinced the professor to let me enroll.

The first day of class, a gentleman stood up and said, "Hi, I'm Clark Gable and I'm legally blind. I need someone to read to me during the class." I raised my hand immediately and said, "I am happy to do it." I needed all the help I could get, and Clark seemed like a bright guy. We met in his office in the library nearly every day; I would read the material to him, and we would discuss it in detail. He helped me understand many concepts that were new to me.

We had one major research paper due in the class that would be our final grade. After grading the papers, the professor listed all the scores on the board—they ranged from 95 percent to 78 percent. I nearly jumped for joy knowing I had passed the class with at least a seventy-eight. When he handed back our papers, I actually had a ninety-two, the second-highest grade in the class.

I have referred to this experience over the years as the Clark Gable principle. If other people can learn something, I can too, even though it may take more work and a mentor like Clark Gable. My success in this class led to a master's degree and then to a PhD. I called on the Clark Gable principle many times while finishing these degrees. I am not sure what path my career would have taken without this propelling event in my life.

This is exactly what is required to shed our fictitious ego. We have to do things that are slightly outside our confidence level and then take a slightly bigger step following each success. Some experts encourage us to set gigantic goals, even if we can't obtain them, but my experience suggests that we achieve great things by taking a series of small steps, each building on the last, until we arrive at a place we never imagined. This is what Salsa Queen did on her road to a new identity. She started selling on Facebook, which was challenging but doable. Next, she went to the farmers' market, then to several grocery stores, and then to a national chain. Going to Kroger first before taking the previous steps would not have worked. This process of change is illustrated in Figure 1-1.

Figure 1-1: Changing the Ego

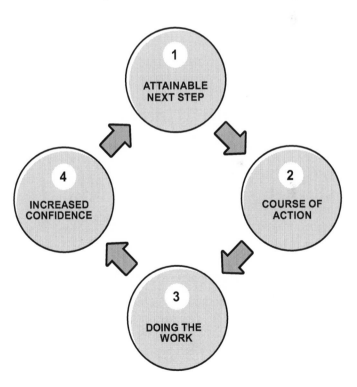

Knowing that we are not our ego and examining our habitual perceptions will only help if we take consistent action. This is what David Durocher meant when he said, "Guys like us change by doing; what that means is acting as if." So if you are ready to lose your old ego, select the perceptions you want to change, choose an attainable step outside your identity, plan a course of action, and do the work. Your increased confidence will lead you to the next step. For example, if you think, "I'm not into fitness but would like to be," start walking, then jogging, then run a 5K, and maybe a 10K. Or if you think, "I wish I had finished college," start with one class, then several classes, then a semester, then graduate. The more of these ego-altering experiences we have, the more we create a new sense of self.

In summary, just as the great teachers taught thousands of years ago—and scholars now agree—we do have an ego or self-identity that develops from our experiences in the external world. Clinging to this fabricated ego sets bounds and limitations on what we do in life. Transcending our ego opens up a whole new world of experiences for us. It gives us a fresh view of ourselves, fosters personal growth, improves our relationships, and leads to greater happiness. As we accept ourselves as "works in progress," we allow others the same privilege and become far less judgmental, which is the next principle in our path to happiness and civility.

Chapter 2

REFRAIN FROM JUDGING

Dora Gae Martin grew up in a small town in Idaho that was 100 percent white. She had everything going for her. She was from the right family, the right religion, the right race, and was the "princess" to her mom and dad. One day while she and a friend were walking home from church, a boy who was five years older pulled up and offered to give them a ride home. They obliged and he took Dora Gae's friend home first. He took a longer way home with Dora who he thought was very attractive. They spent the next ten days together until he shipped out for the Korean War.

Leness Keller was from another small town in Idaho that was thirty minutes away—it, too, was all white. He completed only eight years of school because he was needed on the family farm. He was now on his way to Korea to face some of the fiercest fighting during the war. Two years later on his way home, his ship hit a massive storm. Enormous waves crashed across the deck as the ship rolled from side to side. The bow dropped so deep into the valleys between the waves that the propellers came out of the water. Everyone on board was extremely sick for three days until they reached Puget Sound. "What a thrill it was to be back home for the first time in years."

Dora Gae and Leness dated for several months and then married. Leness didn't have a job but became a very successful entrepreneur. He bought a gas station, started a trucking company, owned a ranch, and served on the hospital board. Their dream was to have six beautiful kids and raise them in small-town Idaho. They ended up with five children—three boys and two girls.

Holly was the third child in the family and the oldest daughter. She became a nurse, worked in the labor and delivery wing of the hospital, and married her best friend, Steve. They desperately wanted children, but after years of trying and several miscarriages, they became disheartened. One day, a doctor Holly worked with called and said, "I just delivered a baby boy, and the mother wants to put him up for adoption. I immediately thought of you and Steve, but you need to know the child is biracial—the mother is Black, and the father is Hispanic. If you are interested, you have thirty minutes to make a decision."

Holly called her mom to discuss this incredible opportunity, which she felt was an answer to her prayers. Dora Gae said, "No! Don't do it! He won't fit in! You'll have nothing but heartache." She feared what family members, friends, neighbors, and her church group might think about white parents raising a Black child. She thought it might damage their family's reputation in the community. Holly and Steve called the doctor back and said yes anyway. They went on to adopt three more biracial and Black children.

This was the first of a double whammy Dora Gae had to face in her conservative, all-white community. The next bombshell dropped when she learned her son Tim was gay. She was convinced this was a choice he was making and had nothing to do with genetics.

So how did Dora Gae come to love her grandchildren more than she ever imagined? How did she learn to accept her son's sexuality and overcome her biases toward the LGBTQ community? How did she become an incredibly loving, accepting, and compassionate woman for the rest of her life?

• • •

Arshay Cooper grew up in a rough neighborhood on the west side of Chicago. The area has been a gateway for immigrants and home to poorer residents of the city. It is a mosaic of African Americans, Puerto Ricans, Mexicans, Polish, Russians, and Greeks. Dilapidated old buildings and filthy vacant lots are the norm, and garbage, debris, liquor bottles, and baggies of drugs litter the streets. Arshay's grandmother moved there decades earlier because her best friend had been hung from a tree in the South.

The neighborhood Arshay grew up in was called the Holy City because every block was home to a different gang whose name ended with the word *Lord*: Insane Vice Lords, Traveling Vice Lords, Renegade Vice Lords. It was essentially a guerilla war zone where the various gangs staged attacks, ambushes, and hit-and-run operations. Arshay had to be very careful that he didn't wear the wrong colors, tilt his hat the wrong way, or accidentally make various gang signs with his hands; if he did, the consequences were dire. By the time he was a teenager, he had run from flying bullets, jumped over pools of blood, and seen dead bodies in the streets.

Not only was the neighborhood broken, but so were many of the families, including Arshay's. His mother, aunts, and uncles were all drug addicts, and so were many of his neighbors. As he walked down the streets and through the hallways of buildings, he was constantly stepping over people in drug-induced fogs—zombie appearances, vacant stares, filthy clothes, howling sounds.

Arshay basically raised himself. He didn't know his dad, and his mom had serious habits. She lost a great deal of weight, roamed the streets, and only came home a couple of times a week. When she was home, she would cry out in the night for her next fix. Arshay had seen other parents die of drug overdoses and he felt his mom would be next. To prepare for this, he held a make-believe funeral in his mind so he could better cope with the inevitable outcome.

Arshay attended Manley High School, one of the most violent schools on the west side at the time. He had to walk through three different gang territories to get there, so he often took the bus to avoid being chased or beaten by gang members. Approximately 600 kids attended the school, but less than 60 percent of the seniors graduated—only 10 percent went to college. The students had to wait in a long line every morning to get through the metal detector at the door, and Arshay had seen the guards confiscate knives, screwdrivers, and box cutters. Three or four gangs were often represented in each class, so the teachers were constantly breaking up fights.

So how did Arshay end up on the first-ever African American rowing team with teammates from various gangs? How did they overcome their biases toward each other and become great friends? And how did they befriend and start rowing with members of the Chicago Police Department?

THE GREAT TEACHERS ON JUDGING

The Hindu Sages

Understanding the Hindu concept of the two selves can help us refrain from judging others. Our false self is an illusion that develops through our communication and experiences with other people— it is not who we really are. Our true self, or atman, has tremendous potential for growth, positive relationships, and genuine happiness.

Once we understand these two selves, we are more likely to detach from our constructed self and see our true human potential. As we do this in our own lives, we are more likely to do it for other people as well. In other words, we become more patient with others because we realize they are simply passing through a stage based on their fabricated self-perceptions. So why would we judge someone today who can be a different person tomorrow, just like we can?

According to Hinduism, our false self will often be confused, mistaken, and highly judgmental of others. In contrast, our true self will be less annoyed, more accepting, and enjoy more satisfying relationships with people.

> The vile are ever prone to detect the faults of others, though they be as small as mustard seeds, and persistently shut their eyes against their own, though they be as large as Vilva fruit.

> Why should you try to mend the failings of the world, sirs? Correct your bodies first, each one of you! Correct your minds first, each one!

> Those who realize the Self enter into the peace that brings complete self-control and perfect patience. They see themselves in everyone and everyone in themselves.

Buddha

Buddha taught his followers to constantly question their perceptions of themselves, other people, and the world in general. He believed that most of our judgments are rather superficial and don't reflect the true nature of people and situations.

> Suppose, monks, that in the last month of the hot season, at high noon, a shimmering mirage appears. A man with good sight would inspect it, ponder it, and carefully investigate it, and it would appear to him to be void, hollow, insubstantial. So too, monks, whatever kind of perception there is, a monk inspects it, ponders it, and carefully investigates it, and it would appear to him to be void, hollow, insubstantial. For what substance could there be in perception?

Buddha taught his followers to refrain from judging other people altogether. He felt we should worry about ourselves first and not perceive or draw attention to the faults of others.

> The faults of others are easily seen, for they are sifted like chaff, but one's own faults are hard to see.

> Do not look at the faults of others, or what others have done or not done; observe what you yourself have done and have not done.

> How do you know the complexity of human character? Do not be a judge of others. Those who judge others only harm themselves.

Jesus Christ

Jesus constantly taught his disciples that judging others was not their role in life. Rather, our focus should be on examining and improving ourselves, not other people. His most impactful teaching on judging occurred during his Sermon on the Mount.

> Judge not, that ye be not judged. For with what judgment ye judge, ye shall be judged: and with what measure ye mete, it shall be measured to you again. And why beholdest thou the mote that is in thy brother's eye, but considerest not the beam that is in thine own eye? Or how wilt thou say to thy brother, Let me pull out the mote out of thine eye; and behold, a beam is in thine own eye? Thou hypocrite, first cast out the beam out of thine own eye; and then shalt thou see more clearly to cast out the mote out of thy brother's eye.

Jesus taught this principle on numerous occasions during his short ministry. After his death, the Apostle Paul continued to teach people to withhold their judgments of others.

> Let us not therefore judge one another anymore: but judge this rather, that no man put a stumbling block or an occasion to fall in his brother's way.

Muhammad

Muhammad also emphasized the harm of making superficial judgments and thinking we are better than other people. In his final sermon, he taught that we should treat each other equally and justly: men and women, Black and white, rich and poor, Arab and non-Arab. He believed that we constantly make assumptions about each other that are incomplete and often not true. According to Muhammad, thinking well of each other is an important part of proper worship.

> How do you judge? Most of them follow nothing but assumptions, but assumptions can be of no value at all against the Truth.

> Believers, no one group of men should jeer at another, who may after all be better than them; no one group of women should jeer at another, who may after all be better than them; do not speak ill of one another; do not use offensive nicknames for one another.

> Happy are those who find fault with themselves instead of finding fault with others.

The Philosophers

Confucius believed we should constantly work on improving our own lives. He felt that examining the foibles of others before considering our own weaknesses is a sign of arrogance and not worth our time or effort. Seneca agreed with Confucius. He felt we should emphasize the inner soul of people, not clothes, jobs, wealth, or social status. Judging people on external factors is like buying a horse after examining only the saddle and bridle, not the animal itself. Although he was one of the richest men in Rome, Seneca regularly invited people of various social classes to dine with him—servants, mule hands, cow herders, and laborers. He was much more interested in their character than the positions they held.

Plato also emphasized the flaws in human judgment. In his Allegory of the Cave, he describes a group of prisoners who have lived in a cave their entire lives. A fire burning behind them is casting shadows on the rock wall in front of them. They erroneously believe the shadows are the real world since this is all they have ever known. One of the prisoners leaves the cave and learns that the real world is far different from the shadowy illusions they have seen all their lives. When he returns to the cave and tells the other prisoners what he has seen, none of them believe him. They are more comfortable clinging to their habitual perceptions than they are exploring a new reality that is foreign to them.

THE SCIENCE ON JUDGING

Decades of research in psychology have shown that we have significant limitations in how we perceive the world around us. As an example, imagine our world is an enormous cathedral adorned with statues, paintings, stained glass windows, and numerous treasures; however, we are not allowed to enter the building. Instead, we only get to see inside through the keyhole in the front door. We can move our head around to get different angles of the main room, but we can never see everything. Yet, we believe we have seen the cathedral.

Human perception works in much the same way. Our brains would suffer serious overload if we tried to process all the stimuli competing for our attention. Research suggests our brains are capable of processing eleven million bits of data per second, but our conscious mind can handle only forty to fifty bits per second. Consequently, we learn to screen some things in and other things out. This is how we survive and make sense of the world. Yet, we believe our incomplete perceptions are reality.

This perceptual process is very active in how we see and evaluate other people. As humans, we are far too complex to understand everything about each other, so we create categories of people to organize our otherwise messy and chaotic world. These categories serve as shortcuts to simplify our interactions, relationships, and decision making. Here are a few of the limiting cognitive processes that operate when we meet and evaluate new people.

Emotional State: People who are happy, kind, and emotionally stable tend to evaluate other people more positively. People who are unhappy, narcissistic, and antisocial are more critical of others and rate them negatively.

First Impressions: Our initial impressions of others, particularly of their face and physical appearance, impact how we evaluate and interact with them. These first impressions remain fairly durable over time and facilitate or impede our effort to develop relationships with people.

Missing Pieces: Once we have initial impressions of people, we tend to fill in other attributes we think are consistent with our limited information. For example, if we perceive people to be attractive, we attribute other positive qualities to their character. If we perceive people to be unattractive, we assign other less desirable qualities to them.

Group Mentality: In addition to filling in the missing pieces, we rely on the assessments of groups we belong to when evaluating other people. For example, if we belong to a political party that seriously dislikes members of another party, we will accept our group's conclusions about the other party's members without doing much investigation on our own.

Perceptual Consistency: Once we have fairly firm perceptions of other people and groups, we tend to focus on future behaviors that reinforce our own conclusions. For example, if we believe someone is intellectually challenged, we will perceive future actions that reinforce this conclusion and miss evidence suggesting the person has unique knowledge or skills.

Self-Projection: We tend to think that people in our various social groups think, believe, and act the same way we do. Hence, we project our thought processes and behavior patterns on them and overlook other unique aspects of their personalities.

Overconfidence: Once our world is nicely organized and people are superficially assigned to categories, we tend to believe that our worldview is accurate. In other words, we are overly confident that we have people and the world figured out.

These cognitive processes lead to inaccurate judgments, stereotyping, and implicit biases. What happens is we observe one or more dominant characteristic of people—race, religion, speech, attractiveness, group membership, and so forth—and then assign a host of additional qualities and put them into one of our categories. Numerous studies show how this unconscious process significantly impacts how we treat and interact with people in a wide variety of settings. Here are just a few findings from the vast research on implicit biases.

Education: Teachers perceive attractive students to be more intelligent than other students. Hence, they spend more time with them, help them succeed, and give them better grades. Teachers also tend to underestimate the abilities of girls and racial minorities. These students are less likely to be tested for gifted programs and more likely to be disciplined and expelled from school.

Health Care: Racial and ethnic minorities receive less attention from doctors, are given fewer diagnostic tests, and experience lower quality of care than white patients. In addition, doctors are less likely to prescribe pain medication for Black patients than for white patients.

Legal System: Biases of police officers lead to more arrests and harsher treatment of racial and ethnic minorities. In addition, the decisions juries and judges make can be influenced by the defendant's race, gender, ethnicity, and religion. Black individuals and ethnic minorities receive more guilty convictions and longer sentences than white defendants.

Finance Industry: We have fewer banks and financial institutions in nonwhite neighborhoods. Consequently, racial minorities lack access to savings and checking accounts and are more likely to use higher-priced check cashing services and payday loans. Racial minorities are also less likely to receive home loans even when they meet the standards for credit worthiness.

The Workplace: Job applicants who are perceived to be attractive and make a positive first impression usually get the job, while many highly qualified candidates get screened out for superficial reasons.

In addition, males are often perceived to be more competent than females, so women are less likely to earn comparable wages, be promoted, and receive leadership roles.

In addition to these biases in institutional settings, we tend to judge people's actions as being either situational or a permanent part of their personality. In other words, people may do things based on a unique situation they are in, but their behavior is not typical of their character. This may occur when people are feeling abnormal stress, being pressured at work, or facing an unfamiliar experience. If we attribute their actions to the situation, we are less likely to develop biases toward them. If we attribute their behavior to their personality, our biases will be much stronger. Research shows that we tend to attribute the actions of people we know and like to the situation but attribute the behavior of strangers to their personality. In other words, we judge people we don't know more harshly.

Here is an example from my college days. One of my professors required us to participate in a training group toward the end of the semester. We spent an entire evening with our fellow students describing how we perceived each other during the class. I was surprised to learn that people thought I was introverted and probably majoring in accounting, math, or statistics; they all assumed I would enjoy working in a cubicle for a large corporation. I actually love music, literature, and the arts and was studying music composition. I also love meeting new people and belonged to several social groups at the time. That's pretty much how the entire evening went. We constructed inaccurate personalities for each other based on limited interaction in a single situation—sitting in a college classroom.

On another occasion, my actions could have been attributed to my personality, but the kind woman I was working with gave me a lot of slack. I was asked to join a community board and assigned to work with Mrs. Lee. Our first experience was going to a training meeting together, and she offered to pick me up at six that morning. I was shocked when the doorbell rang and I had slept through my alarm. This was the first time this had ever happened to me. Blunder number one.

The next experience we had together was visiting an organization in a nearby town. It was my turn to drive. I got lost, and we were late for the meeting. Again, this had only happened to me a few times in my life. Blunder number two.

The third experience was the worst of all. I had just finished a hectic day at work and was racing to our board meeting. On my way there, I noticed my gas gauge was on empty, but I didn't want to stop and be late for the meeting—I couldn't be a flake a third time for Mrs. Lee. I made it on time but then ran out of gas on my way home. I was horrified when Mrs. Lee pulled up behind me to see what was wrong. I told her I had run out of gas, but my wife could come and bring me our gas can. Mrs. Lee wasn't having any of it! "No, no, let's not bother your wife. I will drive you home and bring you back with your gas can." So that's what we did. When we got back to my car, to my horror, I had left my car keys back at my house when I picked up the gas can. It was another half-hour drive to pick up my keys and come back to my car. My third and fourth blunders with the person I had just met a few weeks earlier.

I promise I'm not making this story up! This was one of the only times in my life these things have happened. Everyone who knows me well will tell you I am a well-organized, on-time, type A personality, but this was an unusually hectic time in my life—new job, new city, new baby. So what would you think of me if you were Mrs. Lee? She simply laughed and said, "Things like this happen. It's no big deal," and she never treated me like the bumbling fool I appeared to be. We became very good friends, and I never felt judged by her.

Here is the moral to the story: ever since this experience, I have been a strong proponent of the Mrs. Lee principle, which is, when someone does something stupid, I think it may be a once-in-a-lifetime occurrence, like my four bloopers with Mrs. Lee. I always try to attribute people's behavior to the situation they are in, not their personality. I think Buddha would be pleased with this since he believed we don't have a permanently fixed self anyway, and we will be different people tomorrow, and the next day, and the next day. So why judge people at all?

THE REST OF THE STORY

Shortly after bringing their new baby home, Holly and Steve went to a holiday gathering with Holly's family. Everyone was excited about the baby except for Dora Gae and Leness. According to their daughter Chalon, "It was a chilly meeting. They didn't know if they should be excited or not. They tiptoed around like wolves circling a fire, trying to figure out if this was something they should welcome or not."

Several months later, Holly and Steve had a chance to go to Europe for fifteen days and they asked Dora Gae if she would tend their son. She set up a crib, put a baby seat on the back of her bike, and did the best she could. But when she took the baby to the all-white grocery store in town, everything changed for her. The looks she got ranged from "shock to disgust to disdain." Dora Gae had a decision to make: she could either be embarrassed or become protective. She chose to be protective. She slowly shed her long-held attitude of white pride and decided that "people are people, and if we are going to say we are brothers and sisters, we need to act like it." Here is how Holly described their reunion when she and Steve returned from Europe.

When we picked up our son, my mother had totally fallen in love with him. She had a tenderness about her instead of a cautiousness. Who doesn't fall in love with babies? But it was more than that. She stopped seeing color. With each subsequent adoption, my parents grew more loving to my family. The opportunity to become acquainted with people of color and learn to love them allowed them to become more tolerant and accepting.

This experience changed Dora Gae. She started talking differently, behaving differently, watching different news programs, reading different books, and defending people who were different in her conversations. But she faced another big challenge when she realized her son Tim was gay. All of Tim's siblings knew he was different and couldn't care less, but this was much harder on his parents. They were convinced Tim had made a terrible decision and did everything they could to change him, including therapy and a private school. Tim realized there was nothing for him in small-town Idaho and moved to Florida to get as far away from home as he could.

Dora Gae missed Tim terribly and eventually applied the same lesson she had learned with her grandchildren to her son. According to Chalon, she became much more protective of the LGBTQ community and supported gay rights and relationships—she felt they needed to be loved as well. She even supported more liberal political candidates because she thought people in her area needed to start thinking differently. When Tim later returned to Idaho, he noticed the significant change in his mother.

> Mom was much more approachable. Things were easier, relaxed even. We got along much better, and she seemed genuinely interested in the details of my life. She even met, liked, and cultivated relationships with several of my gay friends.

Tim has stayed in Idaho and has forgiven his parents for the hurt and heartache he experienced in his past. He cared for his father until he died and then cared for his mother full time for seven years until her recent passing. Respectful conversations, increased understanding, and loving actions changed their hearts and minds.

• • •

On one occasion, Arshay Cooper's mother disappeared for a number of weeks. They later found her at the Victory Outreach recovery home. She desperately wanted to overcome her drug habit and change her life. The center was a wonderful mix of Blacks, whites, Puerto Ricans, Mexicans, drug addicts, prostitutes, gang members, and former criminals—all broken-hearted souls. After six months, Arshay's mom came home to her kids and their one-bedroom apartment. She and her daughter shared a sofa bed in the front room, and Arshay and his two brothers slept in the bedroom. His brothers shared an old bunk bed from a thrift store and Arshay slept on a mattress on the floor. Every morning, they had a devotional with songs, scriptures, and prayers, and life got better.

One day at school, a long white boat was displayed with a TV playing scenes of white people rowing the boat. A white woman named Jessica was trying to recruit students to join a new crew team. Arshay's perception of white people was based on stories from his grandmother, and there was no way he was having anything to do with this scheme—putting Black kids who couldn't swim in a boat, no way! But he was impressed with Jessica and her message. He had been raised by women and trusted women more than men, so he decided to give it a try.

The team consisted of rival gang members who hated each other. But as they started having conversations, they realized they were all more alike than they were different. They had all come from difficult backgrounds, they had all been through trauma, and they had joined gangs for belonging and protection. They soon realized their biases toward each other were based on what they had heard about each other, not on actual experiences. The more they talked, the more they understood each other; and the more they understood each other, the more they liked each other. But the thing that brought them together the most was being in the boat.

Once we got out on the water, the same survival mode that told us to run when you hear a gunshot told us that in order to get back to the dock safely, we have to pull for each other. To pull for each other, we have to shut up and listen. We have to do it together, we cannot do it alone, and then you start going as fast as you can. So these biases are not just between white and black, or yellow and brown; they are also between those who look like each other. When we create opportunities to work together, those biases stop.

The team had a similar experience with an all-white team they shared the boathouse with. "We learned to apply the same lessons we learned in the boat outside of the boat." At first, the two teams were leery of each other, but they had a day of service together and started having conversations. They grew to understand each other and learned they had more in common than they realized. "That's when a brotherhood started. In order to find alignment, we have to readjust the lens. We need to talk up close. It is hard to hate up close."

Years later, when the team was making a film about their experience —*A Most Beautiful Thing*—Arshay learned that the thing his teammates' mothers dreaded the most was having their sons interact with the police. Drawing on his past experiences, he felt they could break down these barriers if they rowed and raced with members of the Chicago Police Department. When he brought this up to the film director, she said, "Good luck talking to the guys about this." But they all agreed it was worth a try.

The police had always been strong authority figures in the community and controlled the interaction. Arshay wanted to reverse this dynamic and have his teammates teach the police something they didn't know. He felt this would change their relationship and help eliminate biases on both sides, and this is exactly what happened.

I brought them to the same water where we didn't get along at first, and we truly got a chance to know each other. We learned about each other's strengths and each other's weaknesses. During the training, Alvin, who has done time, sat behind Big Lou, who is a six-foot-four-inch white cop. He didn't know how to swim and was shaking in the boat. Alvin said, "Sit tall, breathe, you belong here," and he started working with him. After every practice, this big cop gravitated toward Alvin every single time. It's all about relationships: learning about the human first. Today, we have a great relationship with those cops, and this makes our block better.

Overcoming biases toward others has been a great gift for Arshay. "It has reduced my fear, I am not afraid of folks, I have learned there are good people everywhere, and I have developed an amazing network." Here is his advice for those of us who want to overcome our tendencies to judge others:

> We don't solve the world's problems by being segregated. We solve the world's problems by working together. If you take time to hear other people's stories, there is light at the end of the tunnel. I always tell people, "Don't expect that tomorrow we are going to have this amazing bridge we are all going to walk across. You can't think it is going to happen tomorrow. What we can do is all lay one brick as perfectly as we can, and then we will have that bridge." But it takes everyone picking up a brick.

THE APPLICATIONS

1. Understand Our Biases

We all develop attitudes in life toward people, groups, things, and experiences. These attitudes become biases when we show prejudice for specific individuals or groups based on incomplete or inaccurate information. Sometimes we understand our biases, and other times we're not even aware they exist. Either way, they can impact our behavior, relationships, and overall happiness.

Our biases are generally based on things like gender, sexual orientation, race, ethnicity, skin color, age, weight, religious preference, or political affiliation. The first step in overcoming unhealthy biases is to examine what they are and where they have come from. Think about adverse attitudes you may have toward groups of people and ask yourself these questions: What information or experiences have led to this bias? How accurate is my information about this group? How is this attitude impacting my behavior?

Identifying our biases is a good start, but it only reveals the ones we know about. A second helpful approach is to sit down with a good friend or partner and ask these questions: "Are there people or groups you feel I have biases toward? If so, can you give me examples from my speech or behavior? How do you think I would benefit from changing this attitude?" Be open, nondefensive, and willing to honestly reflect on what you learn.

A third way to understand our biases is to complete a formal assessment. One of the more popular ones is the Harvard Implicit Association Test, which is available online for free. This evaluation assesses our attitudes toward various groups of people. Complete some of the tests, see where you stand, and review your results with your friend or partner.

Once we have identified our biases, we have to decide if we want to change them. Changing our attitudes requires motivation and effort. If we truly want to grow as individuals, improve our relationships, and increase our happiness, we can make progress. Practicing the steps that follow will help us develop healthier attitudes toward other people.

2. View the World Horizontally

One of the things our egos do is put us on a vertical scale with people. Consequently, we tend to view ourselves as being either above or below other individuals and groups. It is like we are all on a ladder, and when someone moves up a rung, another person moves down. If we view the world this way, we will always have negative attitudes toward other people and groups.

This vertical view of relationships is pervasive in organizations. When I owned a retail company, I loved working in our stores with our team members, most of whom were in their first job. I was constantly impressed by how much these teenagers knew about our customers, their preferences, and how we could improve our business. They became a major source of information for me as I created our plans and strategies.

On one occasion, I was shopping various banks to secure a line of credit to grow the company. A loan officer came to one of our stores and saw me working with our employees during the lunch hour. This was quite concerning to him. He questioned my ability to grow the business because a talented CEO wouldn't spend time doing the menial work of low-level employees. Even though our financials were strong, he denied my application for credit. Sadly, many relationships are damaged and valuable information is lost when we hold a vertical view of life.

A healthier way to view the world is to see people on a horizontal plane. This approach assumes we are all equal, we all have value, and we all have something to contribute. It doesn't put any of us above or below anyone else. This horizontal view is idealistic but attainable with practice. It requires us to overlook external characteristics, refrain from judging, and sincerely desire to learn about other people. Over time, it leads to more friendships, healthier relationships, better solutions, and more civil communities. Figure 2-1 illustrates these two approaches to human relationships.

Figure 2-1: Two Worldviews

VERTICAL VIEW   **HORIZONTAL VIEW**

3. Improve Our Listening Skills

We learn about each other through our communication. Unfortunately, most of us are poor listeners—and we get worse with age. An interesting study shows that 90 percent of first and second graders are able to recall what a teacher has just said. The success rate drops to 44 percent for junior high students and 25 percent for high school students. Adults don't do much better. Following a ten-minute presentation, 50 percent of adults can't describe what was said, and two days later, 75 percent can't even remember the subject.

Part of the problem is our capacity to process information. The average speaker talks at about 125 words per minute, but the brain can process 400 words per minute. This leaves a lot of excess capacity for dwelling on other things during our conversations. If we think we can multitask to fill in the gap, we are wrong. When we multitask, our brain switches back and forth between activities, and we completely space out of one task while focusing on the other. Research also suggests it takes up to 40 percent longer to multitask than it does to do tasks separately.

The invasion of technology is another culprit hampering our listening skills. Next time you are in a meeting or group discussion, notice how many people are looking at their phones, tablets, or computers. A tremendous amount of information is lost when we focus on our smart devices rather than paying attention.

So how can we improve our ability to listen? We can start with a baseline assessment of our current skills. Table 2-1 is a simple evaluation of how well we pay attention in conversations. If you score twenty-five or more, you are a pretty good listener. If you score twenty to twenty-four, you are okay but not great. If you score below twenty, you are a fairly poor listener, like everyone else.

Table 2-1: Listening Assessment

		YES	yes	?	no	NO
1	I usually know what other people are going to say before they say it.	1	2	3	4	5
2	I often pretend to pay attention to people who are speaking when I am really not.	1	2	3	4	5
3	I usually respond immediately when someone has finished talking.	1	2	3	4	5
4	I tend to end conversations that don't interest me by diverting my attention from the speaker.	1	2	3	4	5
5	I generally evaluate what other people are saying while they are saying it.	1	2	3	4	5
6	I usually formulate a response while the other person is still talking.	1	2	3	4	5

The way we listen to other people becomes a habit that repeats itself. Changing our habits takes desire, practice, and time. Learning to truly listen can help us eliminate inaccurate judgments and biases we may have toward individuals and groups. Here are some helpful things we can do to improve our listening skills:

- Put away our technology during our conversations.

- Look directly at the speaker and maintain eye contact.

- Watch for nonverbal cues that convey information.

- Don't judge or interpret while the speaker is talking.

- Ask questions to better understand what is being said.

4. Squelch Negative Communication

"Abracadabra" is a phrase used by magicians just before revealing a magical feat. What they do next is convincing, but it isn't real. Although the origin of the word *abracadabra* is not clear, it appears to be a combination of Aramaic or Hebrew words that mean "I create as I speak." The implication is that we create reality through our communication—and what we create may be accurate, inaccurate, or a total illusion, just like what magicians create.

Research suggests that we do create a social reality for ourselves through our conversations with people. The more we talk about something, the more it becomes real and concrete for us. A fun example of this process appears on *Sesame Street*, one of my favorite shows while my kids were growing up. The two old guys, Waldorf and Statler, are sitting in a box in a theater discussing each act of a play. Table 2-2 shows two conversations they are having. The first one starts positive but ends negative; the second one starts negative but ends positive. They are essentially defining reality during their conversation.

Table 2-2: Communication Forms Attitudes

GOOD TO BAD	BAD TO GOOD
Waldorf: *That was wonderful*	**Statler:** *Boo*
Statler: *Bravo*	**Waldorf:** *Terrible*
Waldorf: *I loved it*	**Statler:** *Bad*
Statler: *Ah, that was great*	**Waldorf:** *Not that bad*
Waldorf: *Well, it was pretty good*	**Statler:** *Ah, pretty good*
Statler: *Well, it wasn't bad*	**Waldorf:** *OK*
Waldorf: *I didn't really like it*	**Statler:** *Decent*
Statler: *It was pretty terrible*	**Waldorf:** *Fair*
Waldorf: *It was bad*	**Statler:** *Great*
Statler: *It was awful*	**Waldorf:** *I loved it*
Waldorf: *It was terrible*	**Statler:** *Bravo*
Statler: *Boo*	

This process not only works for things; it works for people as well. If we talk negatively about individuals or various groups, even if we don't have any interaction with them, our negative attitudes become stronger and more concrete. These attitudes are often inaccurate or complete illusions; it's like we are saying "Abracadabra" before we speak. Consequently, one of the best ways to prevent and eliminate unhealthy biases is to refrain from negative conversations about other people. The advice Thumper got from his parents in the movie *Bambi* is insightful: "If you can't say something nice, don't say nothin' at all." So try going thirty days without saying anything negative about any individuals or groups and see what happens.

5. Engage with People Who Are Different

When our family lived in the Middle East, many of our friends and colleagues were Muslims from Saudi Arabia, Lebanon, Turkey, Kuwait, Egypt, and Syria. This new culture was very different from the one we had experienced in our homogenous hometown in the United States. A few years later, we lived in a wonderfully diverse neighborhood in Atlanta. Our next-door neighbors were from Latin America; the ones across the street were from Pakistan; around the corner were two African American families; and just up the street was a brilliant attorney who worked with prisoners on death row. We were members of our neighborhood HOA, we ate delicious international foods, we visited different churches, and we enjoyed many fascinating conversations.

While growing up, I was taught by a remarkable mother that God loves everyone, that we are all equal, and that no person or group is above or below anyone else. I believed these things but had very few experiences with anyone from a different race, religion, or income level. It's easy to say we care about people who are different when we don't interact with them; it's a whole different experience to live in the same neighborhood, see each other often, and work through challenges together. What I have learned is that we are far more alike than we are different, and we all want the same things in life: health, friends, happiness, loving families, and civil communities.

I think it is difficult to shed our superficial judgments without being around people from different cultures, backgrounds, and beliefs. Examining our biases can change our minds, but befriending people who are different changes our hearts. Learning about other people's experiences, challenges, dreams, and love for their families produces the greatest understanding. Here are some things we can do to overcome our biases and build more satisfying relationships:

- Learn about different faiths and visit their places of worship.

- Volunteer at a local food bank, kitchen, or homeless shelter.

- Befriend people from different cultures and do things together.

- Learn a foreign language and study countries where it is spoken.

- Find an immigrant community and practice your language skills.

- Visit different countries and live like the locals, not the tourists.

In sum, judging other people is part of being human. It's not a character defect of angry, unhappy, or uneducated people—it is something we all do. Our biases develop in much the same way that we form our own self-identity—through early messages we receive from parents, teachers, friends, the media, and our culture. The good news is, we can recognize and change our biases in the same way we can change our limiting self-perceptions.

As we refrain from judging other people, wonderful changes occur in our lives. We are more willing to interact with people who are different, we develop more satisfying relationships, we give people the benefit of the doubt, we strengthen our communities, and we are more inclined to do good deeds for others—which is the next principle in our path to happiness and civility.

Chapter 3

DO GOOD DEEDS DAILY

John Brewer was twenty-three years old when his life changed forever. He was tall and handsome with dark hair and piercing eyes that looked right through you. His great loves were art, music, nature, and especially surfing. He was preparing to move to Hawaii to ride some of the best waves in the world on the day that everything suddenly changed.

John worked as a driver for a company in Santa Monica. He picked up the mail at the post office each morning and took it to the office. On this particular morning, he decided to drive by Venice Beach to check out the waves and see which of his surfing buddies were out early. He saw a green stop light up ahead and continued down the highway. Unfortunately, there was a red light right above him that he missed in the morning sun. A large car going forty miles an hour smashed into his Volkswagen, pushing him through the intersection and into a building. He remembers fighting to stay awake; he thought if he passed out, he would never wake up. His rescuers had to use a blowtorch to cut him out of the car, and his heart stopped at least once.

John woke up in the hospital with a serious spinal cord injury, but he had some sensation in his feet, so he had hope. He was regularly put facedown on a "Stryker board" so he wouldn't get back sores. One day, an orderly flipped the board over but forgot to put the straps on his legs. John crashed to the floor and was knocked out from the impact. When he woke up, he was in "the most intense pain" he had ever experienced. He was put into traction, which helped with the pain, and then given a private room with no visiting restrictions. At times, it was a party atmosphere—the friends and family members who came to visit helped him through this part of his crisis.

After two months of traction in the hospital, John was moved to a rehabilitation center. When he finally realized he would never walk again, the dark cloud of depression struck. He couldn't imagine living the rest of his life in a wheelchair and started contemplating different ways to end his suffering. "It was like a vacuum; the more I thought about it, the more it dragged me down."

One day, a friend of John's named Sticky Jimmy came to see him at the rehab center. His nickname came from a substance he created to hold his feet on a surfboard. John described him as "a big guy with long, long blond hair." Jimmy put John in his car and took him to the beach where they used to surf. Sitting in the sand, John looked over and saw that Jimmy had tears in his eyes, knowing they would never surf together again. John also teared up, which caused a fantastic spectacle of brilliant colors. "Light on the water looked like diamonds, and I realized I was bigger than this. I decided that the physical things in life would not dictate who I am." John knew he could eventually heal emotionally and spiritually, even though he may not heal physically.

Everyone is wrestling with something; my cross was just visible. It turned me inside out, and I had to meet myself. I didn't realize how things like this can build character. It helped me pull on inner strengths, and things I didn't know I had came to the rescue.

Sitting down with John Brewer today is like being with a modern-day sage who constantly exudes marvelous wisdom. In his presence, you feel a deep and genuine brightness that few people possess. So what principles did he discover that came to his rescue? How did he turn dark depression into joyful living?

* * *

Lola Strong had a great family. Her parents taught her the importance of education and hard work. She had the foundation to do great things with her life. "I was very fortunate to have the family I had." So how did she end up living on the streets, addicted to heroin, and in and out of jail and prison?

Lola's father migrated from the Soviet Union to Jordan during World War II because he didn't want to live in a communist country. He met and married Lola's mother in Jordan—her family had also fled from the Soviet Union. The hopeful couple came to America on a boat through Ellis Island in search of the American dream. But life was a struggle in their new country; they didn't speak English and they didn't own a car for the first ten years.

Lola was the youngest of six children. She and her siblings grew up in New Jersey speaking Russian and Arabic. Her parents wanted them to have all the benefits of living in the United States but also wanted to teach them the culture they loved from back home.

> When you opened the door and walked into my house, the culture was different, the food was different, everything was different, nothing was Americanized. When you opened the door and walked out of my house you were in America.

Lola's downward spiral started innocently. She developed a kidney condition in her late teens that was extremely painful. During a hospital stay, she was introduced to opioids. They eliminated the pain and she loved how they made her feel. When her pain finally subsided, her desire to take opioids never went away. She would tell the doctor she was still in intense pain, and he kept giving her the pills. "This may not be fair to say, but my first drug dealer was my doctor, and it wasn't long before I was completely addicted."

Eventually, the doctor caught on to her scheme and stopped prescribing the pills, so she found other ways to get them. She would go to the dentist and complain about severe pain in her teeth. She had several family members who were doctors, and she would steal their prescription pads and write herself prescriptions for opioids. She also learned to call pharmacies and use her family members' DEA numbers to get more prescriptions. This continued for a number of years until someone said to her, "Why are you going to all this trouble when you can just use this." He held up a baggie of white powder and introduced her to heroin. "I was not afraid of it at all.

If it was going to get me high, I was willing to try it, and that was the beginning of the end for me."

Lola started stealing to support her habit. She could no longer hold a job, became estranged from her family, lived on the streets, and at times used her body as an ATM. "I did things that were terrible, and I became a complete monster." Before long, she was doing short stints in the county jail, followed by a series of prison terms.

> When you get out of prison, you think you are going to do something different. But you have no clothes, no job, no car, nowhere to go. You have good intentions, but you are overwhelmed with everything you need to do, and you have no resources. So you end up going back to the only thing you know.

So how did Lola find genuine happiness, improve her relationships, and become part of a remarkable community? How did she start a successful rehabilitation program for addicts, convicted felons, and the homeless? What key principles is she teaching now to save as many lives as she can?

THE GREAT TEACHERS ON GOOD DEEDS

The Hindu Sages

The law of karma underlies the Hindu teachings on good deeds. Karma means "action" and is the universal principle of cause and effect in the world. Every action causes a similar reaction, which becomes the action for another reaction, and the chain continues. Thus, all of our actions, including our thoughts, have consequences due to this web of interconnections. This principle is actually supported by physicists who agree that everything in our world is energy in motion with wavelength properties that ripple around us.

Here is an example of interconnectedness that helps me understand karma. I am sitting at my beautiful desk that was custom built by a talented artist, just for me. He was trained by a talented artist who was trained by another talented artist. The wood came from trees that were planted in a forest, harvested by woodsmen, hauled by truckers, groomed by lumbermen, sold to the artist who crafted my desk, and delivered by a driver to my office. I wouldn't have this attractive desk without all the events that preceded it. A similar pattern of connections occurs for the food we eat, the water we drink, and the knowledge we gain from others. We are all linked in both significant and subtle ways.

The ancient Hindu writings are full of verses on forgetting ourselves, focusing on others, and doing good deeds continually. If we follow this counsel, we will bring good into our lives, discover great wisdom, and find true peace and happiness.

> At the beginning, mankind and the obligation of selfless service were created together. Through selfless service you will always be fruitful and find the fulfillment of your desires.

As a person acts, so he becomes in life. Those who do good become good; those who do harm become bad. Good deeds make one pure; bad deeds make one impure.

Wisdom means a life of selfless service.

The Hindu sages also taught that good deeds should be done for the right reason. For example, it would be a mistake to think that donating money will bring us more money. Rather, we do good deeds to make the world better for everyone. Over time, the consequences of our actions help create the world we are meant to experience.

Those who are motivated only by the fruits of action are miserable, for they are constantly anxious about the results of what they do.

Do such a work in the world whereby everyone will enjoy happiness, peace and cheers.

Buddha

Karma and good deeds are also important themes in Buddha's teachings. He constantly taught his followers to develop a "mind of loving kindness," to have compassion for others, and to treat people the way we would want to be treated.

What is displeasing and disagreeable to me is displeasing and disagreeable to the other too. How can I inflict upon another what is displeasing and disagreeable to me?

Set your heart on doing good. Do it over and over again, and you will be filled with joy.

As a mother watches over her child, willing to risk her own life to protect her only child, so with a boundless heart should one cherish all living beings, suffusing the whole world with unobstructed living kindness.

Our good deeds obviously benefit those we serve: they receive kindness, friendship, food, clothing, shelter, mentoring, knowledge, and so forth. But Buddha also emphasized what we as givers gain from serving others: we sleep well, awaken happy, have serene facial expressions, are liked by others, and rejoice in life. According to Buddha, just as the brightness of the moon far exceeds that of the stars, so do acts of loving kindness far exceed the results of other actions we may pursue in life. "The liberation of the mind by loving kindness surpasses them and shines forth, bright and brilliant." To receive the joy that comes from good deeds, however, we must do them consistently. If we only think about them and talk about them, we will not experience the wonderful outcomes that follow, "just as the cowherd counting other people's cattle cannot taste the milk or ghee."

Jesus Christ

Jesus not only taught the importance of performing good deeds; he was a great example of doing them for his followers. In his short three-year ministry, he taught the multitudes, fed the hungry, comforted the downtrodden, healed the sick, and forgave those who persecuted him. And he constantly taught his disciples to follow his example.

Thou shalt love thy neighbor as thyself.

Whatsoever you would that men should do to you, do ye even so to them.

But he that is greatest among you shall be your servant.

A new commandment I give unto you. That you love one another, as I have loved you.

The story of the Good Samaritan is Christ's most powerful parable on doing good for others. The story was an answer to a question from a "certain lawyer" who asked Jesus, "And who is my neighbor?" Jesus responded that a man traveling from Jerusalem to Jericho was beaten and left half-dead on the road. First, a priest found him and passed on the side. Then a Levite did the same thing. Next, a Samaritan saw the man and had compassion on him. He bound up his wounds, took him to an inn, and cared for him. When he left, he gave the innkeeper money to take care of the man until he returned. Jesus then said to the lawyer and others in the crowd, "Go and do thou likewise."

It is significant that Christ made the Samaritan the good guy in the story. At the time, the Jews felt great animosity toward the

Samaritans—they were the lowly dregs of society. The priest and the Levite would most likely have felt no compassion for the suffering man; it was an early example of class discrimination. The moral of the story is twofold: first, we need to stop judging and despising other groups of people, and second, we need to be like the lowly Samaritan and have compassion for everyone, even those considered our enemies. This was a radical concept at the time.

> Love your enemies, bless them that curse you, do good to them that hate you, and pray for them which despitefully use you, and persecute you.

Finally, just like the Hindu teachings, Jesus taught that we should not perform good deeds to gain recognition or personal rewards. We should do them to truly help people and make our world a better place. "But when thou doest alms, let not thy left hand know what thy right hand doeth."

Muhammad

Muhammad continually emphasized the importance of doing good deeds for others, especially our neighbors. He saw this as a critical practice for peaceful coexistence in the world. He claimed the Angel Gabriel taught him this principle so often that he thought Gabriel might ask us to share our inheritances with our neighbors when we die. Here are a few examples of the hundreds of verses on good deeds in the Qur'an and hadith.

Do good to others as God has done good to you.

None of you is a believer until he loves for his brother what he loves for himself.

Do not regard any act of kindness as insignificant, even if it is only meeting your brother with a cheerful countenance.

Each community has its own direction to which it turns: race to do good deeds and wherever you are, God will bring you together.

Although Muhammad did not teach the law of karma as taught by the Hindus and Buddhists, he did emphasize that our actions have positive and negative consequences. He also taught that doing enough good deeds can compensate for our mistakes and misdeeds in life.

Those who believe and do good deeds will have a reward that never fails.

We shall surely blot out the misdeeds of those who believe and do good deeds.

Muhammad was such a compassionate man he even taught the importance of treating animals kindly. He tells the story of a very thirsty man who descends into a well to get a drink. When he comes up from the well, he sees a dog "lolling out his tongue on account of extreme thirst." He knows what it is like to be thirsty, so he goes back down into the well, fills his shoe with water, climbs back up, and gives the dog a drink. After telling this story, Muhammad's companions asked him, "O Messenger of Allah, are we rewarded for kindness to animals? He responded: There is a reward in doing good to every living animal."

The Philosophers

All of our ancient philosophers emphasized doing good deeds as a premier virtue in life. Aristotle, for example, taught that doing good is essential for becoming good—if we only think about it, we will never achieve our full potential. Seneca agreed with Aristotle; his longest essay was all about giving gifts, favors, and good turns. He was emphatic that giving should occur without any expectation of getting something back. If we give to receive, we are only making a loan and the joy of giving is extinguished. And Thomas Aquinas taught that giving to others is the way we show love for both God and our neighbors. He argued that doing good deeds is critical to perfecting "our deficient inclinations" as humans.

The Chinese philosopher Confucius introduced a wonderful concept he called *ren*, which is much broader than just doing good deeds. *Ren* means compassion, human goodness, warmheartedness, benevolence, and a strong sense of connection to all humanity. Confucius taught that *ren* is the loftiest virtue from which all other virtues follow. He believed that *ren* is critical to achieving true happiness, reaching our full potential as humans, and living civilly together on earth. According to Confucius, *ren* should be the ultimate guide to human conduct for all nations and races.

THE SCIENCE ON GOOD DEEDS

Hundreds of studies have been conducted on the effects of good deeds, volunteerism, and serving others. The results show that the recipients of good deeds obviously benefit: they feel more support, experience less stress, and enjoy greater health and well-being. But what happens to the doers of good deeds? Numerous studies confirm that those who regularly engage in serving others enjoy better physical health, better mental health, and better relationships.

Good Deeds and Physical Health

People who do good deeds and serve others regularly have lower stress levels, more protective antibodies, stronger immune systems, fewer serious illnesses, less frequent pain, better overall physical health, and greater longevity. The findings from this research are impressive. One interesting study shows that people who volunteer have a 44 percent reduction in early death, which is a greater impact than exercising four times a week. Another study shows that high school students who volunteer to help younger students with homework and after-school activities have a greater reduction in various biomarkers for heart disease than students who don't volunteer. These same students also experience lower body mass indexes than their nonvolunteering peers, which is another factor in good health.

An explanation for these impressive results is that doing good deeds helps reduce the stress in our lives. When we experience stressful events, our bodies release various stress hormones, including adrenaline and cortisol. Adrenaline increases our heart rate and blood pressure; cortisol increases sugars in our bloodstream and suppresses our immune system. These chemical reactions are critical when we need to flee from a threatening situation, but they wreak havoc on our bodies if they continue for long periods of time. Ongoing exposure to these hormones can lead to headaches, digestive problems, weight gain, memory impairment, and heart disease. Apparently, serving others shuts down this process and produces substantial physical benefits.

We don't need to experience excessive stress, however, to reap the physical benefits from doing good deeds. Another group of studies shows that whether we are stressed out or not, serving others stimulates the prefrontal lobe of the brain and releases positive hormones like oxytocin, dopamine, serotonin, and endorphins. Oxytocin is a "feel-good" chemical that helps us bond with other people; dopamine creates feelings of pleasure and is used as a medicine to treat heart disease; serotonin is an effective mood stabilizer; and endorphins are the body's natural painkillers. We can all enjoy these attractive outcomes when we serve others.

Good Deeds and Mental Health

People who volunteer and serve others also experience less anxiety and depression, greater emotional stability, higher self-esteem, better work-life balance, more confidence, and greater life satisfaction. As with various physical ailments, the reduction in stress that results from doing good deeds helps produce these positive mental and emotional outcomes.

Apparently, thinking more about other people than ourselves and acting on those impressions stops the mental rumination we all experience over our own challenges in life, which reduces stress and promotes happier emotions. Here is how Dr. Stephen Post, a renowned scholar on the science of good deeds, summarizes the impact of doing good on our overall emotional health.

> All the great spiritual traditions and the field of positive psychology are emphatic on this point—that the best way to get rid of bitterness, anger, rage, jealousy is to do unto others in a positive way. It's as though you somehow have to cast out negative emotions that are clearly associated with stress—cast them out with the help of positive emotions.

Good Deeds and Relationships

In addition to better physical and emotional health, serving other people can significantly improve our relationships. Research shows that people who regularly volunteer and perform good deeds develop new friendships, are more accepting of others, feel a greater sense of belonging, enjoy more satisfying relationships, and have a stronger support network in times of need. Studies also show that people who regularly volunteer can develop better communication and leadership skills. Consequently, they are more employable and have greater success in their careers.

In sum, doing good deeds daily works as a vaccine that reduces stress, improves our physical and mental health, strengthens our relationships, and increases our joy and happiness. However, the strength of these outcomes is influenced by two additional factors. First, several studies show that doing good deeds must actually connect us to other people. Simply donating money to an organization or favorite charity without any human interaction does not produce the same benefits. Second, doing good deeds for personal gain or public recognition reduces the positive effects of serving others. In other words, our motivation for helping people makes a difference in the outcomes we experience. If we feel pressured to help or we serve grudgingly, we will not receive the same good results. Apparently, the age-old counsel of the Hindu sages, Jesus, and Seneca was right on the mark. We should engage in good deeds because we really care about other people and want to make our community better—not because we want specific benefits for ourselves.

I have seen the positive effects of good deeds in the lives of many people during my career. One of my young heroes is a former student named Christian Hobbs. In order to get a job with an impressive corporation, Christian needed to do an internship with one of these companies between his junior and senior years. He was conflicted, however, because we needed someone with his talents that summer to open a new region of our SEED (Small Enterprise

Education & Development) Program in Lima, Peru. He would work with our lending partners, create new curriculum, teach classes in entrepreneurship, and mentor small business owners struggling to climb out of poverty. "I wanted to do something with a human connection that would make the world a better place, and I didn't see that in any of the corporate internships." He accepted our internship, knowing it may cost him an attractive job later.

Christian did a great deal of good that summer in Peru. He taught people concepts to help them increase their household income, raise their standard of living, and send their kids to school. The full impact of his work may not be known for years. "The SEED Program opened my eyes to a completely different world that is almost impossible to experience in the classroom. Nothing in my academic career has been of greater value."

When Christian returned from Peru, he applied for his "dream job" at General Mills in Scottsdale, Arizona. To his surprise, he was selected as one of seven finalists, even though he had not done a corporate internship that summer. "Each finalist was unbelievably qualified. The majority were presidents of their respected organizations, honors students, and accomplished leaders." After several days at the corporate headquarters, the seven candidates were told the final decision would be made in three weeks—this was on a Friday afternoon. On Monday morning, not even a full business day later, Christian received a call from General Mills and was offered the job. When he asked what set him apart from the other unbelievable candidates, they explained without hesitation that it was his experience serving people in Peru—they wanted someone with his passion for doing good in their company. So the choice that he thought would cost him a dream job was the reason he got the job.

> I've been promoted twice and keep making more money, but I am not any happier. What makes me truly happy is serving others and building things that have value. I will forever be grateful for the lessons I learned, the friends I made, and the experiences I had in Peru. It was the perfect platform to launch me into my future.

Another friend of mine believes that doing good deeds saved his marriage. Richard Paul Evans is a *New York Times* and *USA Today* bestselling author with more than 20 million copies of his books in print. As his career progressed, the pressures of his newfound fame and fortune put a huge strain on his marriage. He and his wife, Keri, were fighting so much that going out on book tours was a huge relief for Richard, but they both paid a huge price when he returned home.

The crisis hit a boiling point one night while Richard was at the Ritz-Carlton in Atlanta. He and Keri had a major clash during a phone call, and Keri hung up on him. Richard wasn't sure it was possible to save their marriage and was extremely distraught. As he was standing in the shower "yelling at God" that he couldn't do it anymore, he had a powerful impression: "You can't change her,

Rick. You can only change yourself." When he returned home, he knew what he had to do.

The next morning, he asked Keri, "What can I do to make your day better?" In shock, she replied, "Why are you asking that?" "Because I mean it," he said. "I just want to know what I can do to make your day better." Her cynical response was, "Go clean the kitchen," which he did. The next morning, he asked the same question, "What can I do to make your day better?" Keri's reply this time was, "Clean the garage," which he did for the next two hours.

Richard continued to ask Keri this question every morning, and it was during the second week that "a miracle happened." Keri broke down and started crying, telling him she felt she was the problem. "I am hard to live with; I don't know why you stay with me." "It's because I love you," he said. "What can I do to make your day better?"

Richard asked Keri the same question every day for more than a month. His daily deeds softened both of their hearts, and the bitter walls came crashing down. They started talking more, spending more time together, and the fighting stopped. Then Keri started asking, "What do you need from me?" They both feel that good deeds saved their marriage.

> I not only love my wife; I like her. I like being with her. I crave her. I need her. Many of our differences have become strengths and the others

don't really matter. We've learned how to take care of each other and, more importantly, we've gained the desire to do so.

THE REST OF THE STORY

After John Brewer's trip to the beach with Sticky Jimmy, he knew what he had to do. He started thinking more about other people's happiness than the hard hand life had dealt him. He tried to be the best patient he could possibly be, he worked hard in therapy, and told his health care providers how much he loved and appreciated them. When people came to visit him, he would "put on a smiley face" even if he didn't feel good and ask them about their lives. He wanted them to have a positive experience with him and know he was going to be okay.

> I could have just pulled the covers over my head and closed my eyes until it all went away—a lot of people like me do that. But then I started focusing on the people who were serving me, and things started to turn around. It was not about me anymore but about the people around me.

John's road to recovery was long and challenging. He learned to sit up in his wheelchair, push himself around, drive a car with hand controls, and he went back to college. He graduated with a degree in art and became a high school teacher. He was such a positive and caring person that everyone loved him and wanted to hang out with him. He would regularly show up at parties with a van full of "new friends" he had made. In time, he married his beautiful wife, Annie, and they had four remarkable children.

During his recovery, John needed something to burn off the high-octane energy he had as a surfer before his injury. He started pushing his wheelchair around his neighborhood and eventually registered for a full 26.2-mile marathon. The race director was skeptical that he could finish the event, so he followed him along the entire route. John was one of the first people in the country to complete a full marathon in a wheelchair. He went on to pioneer the sport and help many people recover from spinal cord injuries.

John has now completed 150 marathons, 48 half-marathons, 70 10Ks, and 4 ultramarathons. He has also won gold and silver medals in the world Paralympic Games. His commitment to focus on other people has made all the difference in his extraordinary life.

Focusing on others had such a big impact on me that it directed my life's work as a teacher. You hear about teachers who get really burned out, but the more I taught and the more I gave, it just got sweeter and sweeter for me. When you think more about other people's happiness than your own, it really does make you happier. So when people say "thank you" to me, I say "thank us" because we are doing this together. Better me for a better you for a better me. Now I feel so much love.

· · ·

When Lola received a five-year prison term for her fifth conviction, she contacted Delancey Street—the same organization that saved David Durocher's life. She knew the program was long and hard, but she was disgusted with herself and knew if she went back to prison, she would continue on the same vicious cycle of failure. Delancey Street accepted her into the program, but the judge didn't want to release her—he was convinced she would fail. She begged him to give her a chance and he finally conceded, but he told her that when she failed, she would serve every day of her five-year sentence.

The first person Lola met at Delancey Street was a woman she knew from the streets. She had used drugs with her and spent time with her in prison. This woman had been at Delancey Street for four years.

> It was amazing to me because she was so different. I was so flabbergasted at the change in her that it was an instant gift for me. I knew that if she could change, I could change, too. That's all I needed. I made a commitment to do everything they asked of me and put 100 percent into the program, and that's what I did.

Lola slowly started to change, but it was hard work. She learned to accept feedback, take responsibility for herself, and help other people—which was a key factor in her recovery. Serving others is a critical part of the therapy at Delancey Street; hence the oft-quoted motto, "When person A helps person B, person A gets better." From your first week in the program, you are given the opportunity to serve. First, you become a welcomer and orient new people to the facility. Next, you become a mentor, a tribe aid, a tribe leader, and a barber—not the kind that gives haircuts but someone who reprimands those who break the rules.

Lola was made a crew boss at six months and didn't feel worthy or prepared for the responsibility. "It turned out to be the best thing that ever happened to me because I grew so much." She was able to "get outside of herself" and mentor other women who were struggling to succeed in the program. She knew that if she could change, anyone could change.

> Helping other people became a new high for me. It made me feel good about who I was. I took all the horrible things I had done and used them to restore hope in other people. Serving other people helped me realize I had value.

After her successful stay at Delancey Street, Lola helped start The Other Side Academy in Salt Lake City. Their motto is, "When you get to The Other Side Academy you are no longer part of the problem, you are part of the solution; we all help each other succeed." The residents cook the food, clean the house, do the laundry, and work in the businesses the organization operates—a moving company, thrift boutiques, food trucks, and a construction company. "Everybody contributes down to the newest person in the house—it's like a machine that just works on its own."

Once the Salt Lake facility was operating effectively, Lola moved to Denver and opened a new branch of The Other Side Academy there. Her dream is to continue opening facilities across the country and save as many lives as she can. Her intense focus on helping others has made her happier than she has ever been.

I think everyone should have a job where they serve other people. It's the best thing in the world, especially coming from someone like me who spent twenty years of my life as a selfish taker. My passion now is helping people find hope, find what they are good at, and find their purpose in life. I am really fulfilled right now. I can't remember a happier time than helping to launch The Other Side Academy. It's full steam ahead; we're going to save a lot of lives.

THE APPLICATIONS

1. Just Do It

Every day presents numerous opportunities for doing good deeds if we watch for them. We can help our family members, friends, neighbors, and colleagues at work. These can be simple and unplanned acts of kindness like making breakfast, going to the store, buying lunch, giving a compliment, writing a letter, making a phone call, helping with a problem, cleaning up a workspace, mowing a lawn, shoveling snow, and on and on.

We can also do good deeds for people we don't know throughout our day: things like smiling, holding a door, giving directions, carrying a package, buying a meal, paying a bill, sharing an umbrella, and so forth. Based on the research we reviewed above, this will release the "feel-good" chemicals in our bodies and minds and improve our happiness and relationships. And the more we do good deeds, the more they will become a natural part of our character.

So let me challenge all of us to an experiment. Let's start each day asking ourselves, "Who can I help today?" The answer may come in prayer, meditation, or in quiet reflection each morning. I am a strong believer that impressions come to us more clearly when we want to help other people than when we want to benefit ourselves—it has something to do with the flow of intelligence in the universe. Next, let's commit to doing at least one good deed for someone each day for a month and see what happens. Let's keep a journal of what we do and how we feel about each experience. I am confident we will want to continue doing good deeds after a month. If we don't, we will miss out on the joy of thinking about others more than ourselves.

2. Meet Specific Needs

In addition to doing random good deeds each day, specific people, groups, and organizations always need help. Committing to a more structured plan of giving keeps us doing good deeds on a regular basis. Do you know a person who needs continual help and support? Perhaps a child that needs mentoring, a neighbor with a long-term illness, a family that has lost a loved one, an aging parent, or a friend going through a divorce. Scheduling ongoing time to help someone blesses his or her life as well as our own. This is what Richard Paul Evans did when he committed to do something for his wife each day to make her life better—which saved their marriage.

Along with helping specific people, every city has organizations that need regular volunteers: the American Red Cross, Big Brothers Big Sisters, Habitat for Humanity, Volunteers of America, the local food bank, and so on. I suggest you find an organization that is working on a problem you are excited to help solve like literacy, hunger, poverty, homelessness, and so forth. When we do things we are passionate about, it strengthens our motivation and commitment to serve. This is what Christian Hobbs did when he joined our SEED Program to help people rise out of poverty through entrepreneurship. You can find a number of opportunities in every city across the country on websites that link volunteers with service opportunities. I suggest you try volunteering for a few months and see what happens. As the research suggests, people who volunteer develop new friends, feel a sense of belonging, enjoy better relationships, have a stronger support network, gain valuable skills, and do well in their careers.

3. Be an Advocate for Ren

Doing any of the above is more than adequate to increase our happiness and make a difference in our community. At some point, however, we may find ourselves in a role that provides an opportunity to promote *ren* more broadly. For example, many of the new age entrepreneurs I have worked with during my career have added a social initiative to their business. In addition to creating great products and services, they want to give back to the community in which they operate. One company allows its team members to do service projects in the community during their off season and still get paid. Another young entrepreneur uses a percentage of his profits to build schools and promote literacy. Others volunteer to teach in schools, mentor students, and support programs for at-risk youth.

When we are in any kind of leadership role—teacher, coach, manager, neighborhood leader, or parent—we can organize projects that promote *ren*. This will help solve recurring problems, strengthen our communities, and expose even more people to the joy of doing good deeds. Personally, I think volunteering and serving others should be promoted by all types of organizations as a healthy lifestyle. The more of us involved in doing good, the more the chain reaction expands, and the more perpetual good deeds become a natural part of our culture. This is definitely an outcome worth pursuing.

In sum, in the bestselling novel *Pay It Forward*, a young boy creates an ingenious plan for changing the world. He commits to help three people, who in turn will help three people, who will also help three people, and so on. The math shows that eventually the entire world will be impacted by good deeds, much like a virus can infect the world. Although this is a great story, some evidence supports the underlying assumption that "emotional contagion" is possible. Proponents of this theory cite the "laughing epidemic" in Tanzania in 1962. It started with several girls laughing uncontrollably at a boarding school and quickly spread to 95 of the 159 students. It continued spreading for months, eventually infecting nearly 1,000 people at fourteen different schools, which all had to close for a brief period to control the strange epidemic. Although several researchers surmise this was a reaction to stress the children were feeling, the laughter still spread from person to person to person.

Likewise, if we help other people, they are more inclined to help other people, who are also more inclined to help other people, and the results grow exponentially. Apparently, kindness is contagious. According to the law of karma, the goodness we spread will eventually flow back into our own lives, even though this was not our original intent for doing good. Research strongly supports this outcome: helping others can significantly improve our health, emotions, relationships, and overall happiness. "When person A helps person B, person A gets better."

We have now talked about transcending our fabricated sense of self, withholding judgment of others, and increasing the good deeds we do for our fellow sojourners on earth. This is all awesome, but as we increase our interaction with other people, we are also more likely to offend one another. Forgiving each other for these offenses is the next principle in our path to happiness and civility.

Chapter 4

FORGIVE
ONE ANOTHER

Zach Snarr was bigger than life, with an infectious sense of humor, and a love for practical jokes. Everyone who knew him loved him. He and Yvette Rodier had been friends for years. They were in the same classes in high school, and when she entered the room, he always had a smart-alecky remark for her. She actually looked forward to his creative comments.

Zach and Yvette had their first date alone on a stunning summer night in August. After dinner at an Italian restaurant, they drove up the canyon to photograph the full moon over the reservoir. While they set up the tripod and camera, a white truck pulled into the parking area and the driver walked down the path to the lake. He asked Yvette where the trail went, and she replied, "I don't know. We haven't been here." The man then pulled out a gun and shot Zach and Yvette multiple times.

Zach was hit twice in the head and once in the abdomen and died instantly. Yvette was hit several times but was still alive. As she lay there screaming, the man reloaded his gun and shot her again. She was hit multiple times in the head, twice in her torso, once in her shoulder, and once in her leg. Still conscious, she played dead with her eyes open because that's what she thought a dead person would look like. As the shooter went through her pockets, she could feel his breath on her face. He then went through Zach's pockets and took his wallet and car keys.

Jorge Benvenuto was a nineteen-year-old immigrant from Uruguay with emotional challenges. He decided he no longer wanted to live but was afraid to take his life. He thought if he did something really horrible, he would have the courage to kill himself—that was his plan that night. After going through Zach's and Yvette's pockets, he walked back up the trail and drove away in Zach's car, leaving his truck at the scene.

When Yvette heard the car pull away, she called out Zach's name, but the moon-filled night was completely silent. She knew the shortest way to get help was to climb up the mountainside to the road, so she crawled up a steep incline through rocks, brush, and trees. When she finally reached the road, a couple driving along the reservoir nearly ran her over. The driver recalled, "She was a mass of blood. It looked like a horror movie. She had more holes than we had hands." They stayed with her until the police arrived and a helicopter flew her to a local hospital.

The knock on the Snarrs' door came at 12:45 a.m. Two detectives told Zach's parents—Ron and Sy—that Zach had been shot and killed. They couldn't believe it at first, but then the horror sunk in. When they learned that Yvette had also been shot but was still alive, Sy responded, "I have to go see her." When she arrived at the hospital a few hours later, she told Yvette, "We are glad you are still alive," and they hugged and wept.

Several days later, Jorge Benvenuto was apprehended at a gas station. He still hadn't found the nerve to take his life. During a long and drawn-out legal process, he eventually pleaded guilty and was given life in prison without the possibility of parole.

For seventeen years, Ron and Sy suffered from intense anger and despair. They hated Jorge Benvenuto, his family, and all the attorneys who represented him. According to Sy:

> It was like a cancer spreading through my whole body. I wanted to hurt him like he hurt Zach. I would look around and see all these people getting on with their lives and think, *How can they be happy? How can they laugh?* For me, life was basically over.

So how did Ron and Sy survive this unimaginable tragedy? How did they overcome their anger and hatred toward Jorge? How did they become great friends with his family? A series of unexpected steps helped them to forgive, heal, and love again.

* * *

> I was really supposed to die—that was the ultimate objective—but I was young and very strong, so I was always put to work.

Henri Landwirth grew up in Poland. When he was thirteen years old, his family was rounded up and taken to a concentration camp because they were Jewish. Over the next five years, he experienced five different camps, one of them being Auschwitz.

Henri's father was killed early on. German soldiers marched him out of the camp with other prisoners and shot him in the head; he was buried in a mass grave. His mother lived nearly five years after being captured. Just before the war ended, soldiers put her on a boat with other female prisoners and exploded the boat with dynamite. All of the women died except for a Polish girl who was an Olympic swimmer. Henri met her later and learned more about his mother's life in the camp.

> The most difficult thing about the camps was the hunger and thirst I had to live with daily. You think about food constantly and become like an animal. Some prisoners were so hungry they ate the infected food of those who died of typhoid, just for the sake of feeling full for once. I did this myself one time and became very ill. I was taken to the hospital, something the guards only did when a prisoner was dying. When I woke up the next morning, everyone was dead but me, so they sent me back to the camp.

Toward the end of the war, Henri and a group of prisoners were marched out of the camp. Henri understood German, so he knew the soldiers had been ordered to shoot them. "I was surprised at the depth to which I did not care; I just couldn't take it anymore. The other prisoners also seemed pleased that the end was here." When they reached the forest, one of the soldiers said to his comrades,

"The war is almost over, and I don't want to kill these people." The other soldiers didn't seem to care, so he said to the prisoners, "Line up over there facing the trees. When I raise my gun, run into the woods."

Henri ran for about a mile and then started walking. For the next few weeks, he wandered from village to village, stealing food and trying to stay hidden. One day, he found an abandoned house on the outskirts of a small town and went inside and fell asleep. He was awakened by an older woman who told him he was in Czechoslovakia and the war was over.

The next few years were extremely difficult for Henri. He had only a sixth-grade education and had missed all of the normal experiences a young boy has from thirteen to eighteen years old. He had no family, no skills, and a terribly painful past that impacted his thoughts and behavior. He went to Belgium but struggled to survive.

> Many times, I slept through breakfast because there was nothing to eat—it was that bad! I was alone, discouraged, and wanted to leave Europe because the memories were too difficult. So I came to the United States with $20 in my pocket.

How does someone like Henri escape his dreadful past, move forward, and find lasting happiness in life? How does he go on to build the world's largest nonprofit organization for children with terminal illnesses, Give Kids the World? Learning to forgive and serve others were huge factors in his healing.

THE GREAT TEACHERS
ON FORGIVENESS

The Hindu Sages

The Hindu sages taught that forgiveness and reconciliation are important to peace and happiness in life. Holding grudges is characteristic of the lowest form of consciousness referred to as tamas. When tamas dominates our thinking, we live in a state of darkness, delusion, and confusion. In contrast, forgiveness is part of the highest state of consciousness called sattva. When we achieve sattva, we enjoy peace, light, and harmony in our relationships. Sattva is like a delicious nectar that "binds us to happiness."

People who are truly forgiving of others are considered heroes in Hindu life. They also enjoy a "supreme peace of mind" and are unaffected by those who seek to hurt or offend them.

If you want to see the brave, look to those who can return love for hatred. If you want to see the heroic, look to those who can forgive.

Forgiveness subdues (all) in this world; what is there that forgiveness cannot achieve? What can a wicked person do unto him who carries the saber of forgiveness in his hand? Fire falling on the grassless ground is extinguished of itself. (But) an unforgiving individual defiles himself with many enormities. Righteousness is the one highest good; and forgiveness is the one supreme peace.

Buddha

Buddha taught that there are three types of people who respond to offenses in life. The first is like a line etched in stone. The second is like a line etched in the ground. The third is like a line etched in water.

> And what kind of person is like a line etched in stone? Here, some person often gets angry, and his anger persists for a long time. Just as a line etched in stone is not quickly erased by the wind and water but persists for a long time.

> And what kind of person is like a line etched in the ground? Here, some person often gets angry, but his anger does not persist for a long time. Just as a line etched in the ground is quickly erased by the wind and water and does not persist for a long time.

> And what kind of person is like a line etched in water? Here, some person, even when spoken to roughly and harshly, in disagreeable ways, remains on friendly terms with his antagonist, mingles with him, and greets him. Just as a line etched in water quickly disappears and does not persist for a long time.

According to Buddha, people like a line etched in water enjoy healthier relationships and greater happiness than people who are quick to anger and hold grudges for long periods of time. He also taught that it's foolish to cling to any lasting perceptions of ourselves and others since we are all constantly changing—we will all be different people tomorrow than we are today. Consequently, we should view each other as works in progress and freely forgive when offenses occur. Even though this is hard to do, it leads to the greatest peace of mind.

> When an angry person is overcome and oppressed by anger, though he may sleep on a couch spread with rugs, blankets, and covers, with an excellent covering of antelope hide, with a canopy and red bolsters at both ends, he still sleeps badly.

> One who repays an angry man with anger thereby makes things worse for himself. Not repaying an angry man with anger, one wins a battle hard to win.

Jesus Christ

Jesus emphasized two types of forgiveness during his ministry. First is the forgiveness that God offers all of us as we strive to change and improve our lives. Second is the forgiveness we are asked to offer others who commit offenses against us. In other words, God is willing to forgive us for an entire lifetime of mistakes and errors, and he wants us to likewise forgive one another.

> Whosoever shall smite thee of the right cheek turn to him the other also.

> Love your enemies, bless them that curse you, do good to them that hate you, and pray for them which despitefully use you and persecute you.

For if you forgive men their trespasses, your heavenly Father will also forgive you.

Jesus emphasized his principle of forgiveness in his parable of the unforgiving servant. This parable came about in response to Peter's question, "How oft shall my brother sin against me, and I forgive him? Till seven times?" Jesus answered, "Until seventy times seven," and then he recited the following story.

A wealthy king took account of his servants, and one of them owed him 10,000 talents. The king threatened to sell the man and his family if he did not pay the debt. Biblical scholars agree that 10,000 talents were far more than the servant could pay back in multiple lifetimes. Hence, the servant fell down at the feet of the king and begged for mercy. The king was moved with compassion and forgave the entire debt.

Next, the servant approached one of his fellow servants who owed him one hundred pence, which was a few months' wages. This man was unable to pay the debt, so the servant had him cast into prison. When the king heard this story, he sent for the servant and said, "I forgave thee all that debt because thou desiredst me: Shouldest not thou also have had compassion on thy fellow servant, even as I had pity on thee?" The king then delivered the servant to the tormentors until he paid off his debt.

It doesn't matter if the offenses against us are petty or great. Failing to forgive others is inconsistent with the infinite forgiveness of God. Christ was the greatest example of this principle as he hung on the cross and uttered the words, "Father, forgive them; for they know not what they do."

Muhammad

Muhammad taught the same two types of forgiveness emphasized by Christ: God is generous and quick to forgive, and we must learn to forgive others. The phrase "God is most forgiving and merciful" appears over and over again in the Qur'an. In addition, numerous verses in both the Qur'an and the hadith extoll the virtue of forgiving others.

> Kind words and forgiveness is better than a charitable deed followed by hurtful words.

> The most virtuous of virtues is to connect and have good relations with those who cut you off, to give to those who deny you, and to overlook and pardon those who revile or falsely accuse you.

> O Messenger of Allah, how many times should a servant be pardoned? He said: Seventy times a day.

Like Jesus, Muhammad emphasized the principle of forgiveness in stories. One of these is the story of Joseph being sold into Egypt by his brothers, which also appears in the Old Testament in the Bible. When a famine occurred in the land, Jacob sent his sons who had sold Joseph to Egypt to obtain food and supplies for the family. Since being sold, Joseph had been a slave, a prisoner, and was now managing pharaoh's storehouse. His brothers knew they had committed a grave error and were afraid they would not be forgiven. But Joseph freely forgave them, brought the entire household of Jacob to Egypt, and provided them with food and safety.

On another occasion, a relative of Muhammad's wife was spreading rumors about her. Her father swore he would never again provide any kind of support for this relative. On hearing this news, Muhammad uttered these words:

> Those who have been graced with bounty and plenty should not swear that they will no longer give to kinsmen, the poor, those who emigrated in God's way: let them pardon and forgive. Do you not wish that God should forgive you? God is most forgiving and merciful.

The Philosophers

The Greek philosophers generally didn't refer to forgiveness as a primary virtue but as an outcome of other virtues like being magnanimous, good-tempered, and high minded. According to Aristotle, "A good-tempered man is not disposed to take vengeance but rather to pardon. Nor will he bear grudges; for it is the mark of a high-minded man not to bring up the past, especially what was bad, but rather to overlook this." Aristotle believed that forgiving offenses was a highly desirable quality but had little to do with the person being forgiven. Holding petty grudges or being vindictive was simply below the dignity of a magnanimous individual.

Thomas Aquinas, who spent his life merging Aristotle's philosophy with Christian theology, agreed with Aristotle's concept of forgiveness but took it one step further. He believed that every member of a community is a part of the whole and that individual actions can affect the entire community. Just as God seeks us out and freely forgives our offenses, Aquinas believed that we should actively seek our offenders and achieve reconciliation. This is true forgiveness that benefits the individuals and the community.

Confucius was a huge proponent of compassion, kindness, and positive relationships. Hence, forgiveness was something he talked about often. Here are a few of his more popular sayings:

To be wronged is nothing unless you continue to remember it.

Those who cannot forgive others break the bridge over which they themselves must pass.

If you are exacting with yourself but forgiving to others, then you will put enmity at a distance.

THE SCIENCE
ON FORGIVENESS

Hundreds of studies have been conducted on the concept of forgiveness. It may be the most thoroughly researched principle in the path to happiness and civility. Robert Enright, a professor at the University of Wisconsin, is considered the pioneer of forgiveness research and has conducted more than one hundred studies himself. In addition, institutes and university centers have been established to study and teach the practice of forgiveness. Here are some of the conclusions from several decades of research:

- Forgiveness can significantly reduce underlying stress in our lives.

- Forgiveness lowers anxiety, depression, and other emotional disorders.

- Forgiveness can reduce blood pressure and the risk of heart disease.

- Forgiveness improves peace of mind and the quality of our sleep.

- Forgiveness helps heal marriages adversely impacted by infidelity.

- Forgiveness reduces PTSD for people who have experienced abuse.

- Forgiveness helps substance abusers reduce their frequency of drug use.

- Forgiveness lowers anger, resentment, and revenge in the workplace.

- Forgiveness leads to more satisfying relationships in families and at work.

- Forgiveness increases a sense of empowerment and control over our lives.

The science is clear: harboring grudges and refusing to forgive others results in anger, hurt feelings, and embedded anxiety—and it's these negative emotions that do the damage to our mind, body, and relationships. Here is an analogy: A few weeks ago, our dishwasher flooded the kitchen floor. From past experience, I knew I had to fix it quickly. If it continued to flood, it would damage the floor, seep through to the basement ceiling, destroy the sheetrock, damage the light fixture, spill onto our pool table, warp the wood, leak onto the basement floor, and damage the carpet. I would have a huge, expensive mess to clean up. The same thing happens when we hold on to anger and grudges. The negative emotions continue to spread and harm us emotionally, socially, and biologically. But when we learn to forgive and let go quickly, these negative emotions dissipate, and we enjoy the positive outcomes of forgiveness highlighted in the research above.

Obviously, some of us have an easier time forgiving than others; and some of us have far greater offenses to forgive than others—like Ron and Sy Snarr and Henri Landwirth. The good news is, we can all develop this attribute in our lives if we are willing to invest the time and effort. Research has shown that forgiveness training can help a wide variety of people—victims of abuse, cardiac patients, the terminally ill, substance abusers, students who have been bullied, and many others—learn to forgive and enjoy greater emotional and physical health. So the benefits of forgiveness are available to everyone.

I have witnessed the power of heroic forgiveness a number of times in my life. Here's an experience that had a major impact on our family and community. On a cold February night, we learned that our son's friend, Michael Williams, had just lost half of his family in a tragic automobile accident. Michael's parents, Chris and Michelle, were out with three of their children, Ben, Anna, and Sam, when they were hit by a seventeen-year-old drunk driver. Michael was not with them that night.

Chris was the only one conscious after the crash. He looked over at Michelle in the passenger seat, felt for a pulse, and knew that she and their unborn child were dead—Michelle was five months pregnant. Next, he looked at Ben in the back seat. He had a large gash on his head that exposed his skull. There was no blood coming from the wound, so he knew Ben was also dead. Anna was in the middle back seat and Sam was directly behind him. He wasn't sure what condition they were in but later learned that Anna was dead and Sam was alive.

As Chris sat in the car injured, waiting for help, he saw the car that hit them. At that moment, he heard a clear voice in his mind that said, "Let it go," and he knew what it meant. He had just lost his wife and two of his children and was about to face the most difficult challenge of his life. He couldn't add to that heavy burden the weight of hating the driver who hit them. He committed to not pick up that burden even though he had no idea who the driver was or what had caused the accident.

Chris later learned that the seventeen-year-old boy who hit his family had been drinking that night. He learned that the boy's parents lived a few houses away from Michelle's parents; he learned that the boy's siblings lived in his neighborhood; and he learned that the boy's uncle was one of the physicians who treated Sam at the hospital. Chris remained firmly committed to the decision he made the night of the accident to "let it go" and forgive the driver who caused the accident. "I felt no anger, no desire for retribution or justice, no questioning as to why this happened."

The media was very interested in the accident and Chris's commitment to forgive the young teenage driver. Chris decided to hold a brief press conference to address all of the requests for interviews he was receiving. Here is one of the things he said:

On behalf of my sweet wife, our children, and my extended family, we would invite you if you are in a position to extend a single act of kindness, a token of mercy, or an expression of forgiveness. Would you do it by Valentine's Day and then, if you feel to do so, write that experience down and share it with my two surviving boys. I can think of no greater valentine that you could give to someone.

Chris and his two sons received thousands of letters and emails from people all over the world describing acts of forgiveness, kindness, and charity. Many people described how rewarding and freeing their experiences were. A general theme of these letters and emails was, "If you can forgive someone for doing that to your family, certainly I can forgive."

A year after the accident, Chris met Cameron, the young boy who had killed his wife and two children, for the first time. They have developed a compassionate relationship, and Chris has helped Cameron forgive himself and move on with his life. This experience has helped Chris develop a much deeper joy and happiness than he thought was possible after the tragedy.

THE REST OF THE STORY

After seventeen years of debilitating hatred, a series of small miracles happened to Sy Snarr. First, a woman gave a talk at their church about a family whose loved one had been murdered, and how they eventually forgave the offender. "Her talk changed me. I just sat there weeping and thinking, *I would love to feel something again other than all this hatred and anger I carry.*"

Second, Sy could see what her hatred was doing to her children. One day, she was sitting in the living room thinking about Zach and she started sobbing. She looked up and saw her oldest son, Trent, staring at her. "He looked so sad and just walked out of the room. I thought, *What am I doing to my kids?* I love them as much as I love Zach, and I knew I needed to let it go."

Next, after twenty-one years, Jorge wrote a letter to Sy, but he sent it to his mother. He wanted her to deliver it in person, but she kept it for a year because she wasn't sure Sy would want to read it. The letter eventually got to Sy through a circuitous route, and she and Ron read it together.

It was the most amazing letter. He didn't make any excuses. He took full responsibility and said, "Please don't blame my family for my actions; they are good and decent people who feel nothing but sorrow and regret for what you have gone through. I am so sorry for taking away Zach's right to life, your time with him, and whatever God had planned for him." It was just the most beautiful letter and I knew it was sincere. I felt every last bit of hatred just leave me.

She and Jorge—who now prefers to be called George—started writing every month, then twice a month, and then every week. At first, they signed their letters "Sincerely, Sy" and "Sincerely, George." Before long, they were signing them "Love, Sy" and Love, George." Eventually, they decided they wanted to meet in person and Sy was approved for the visit. She went to the prison in February 2020, just before it was closed to visitors due to the COVID-19 pandemic.

The victims' services coordinator told Sy they could spend up to two hours together, but he thought the visit might only last fifteen minutes because "George is very quiet." Sy was shocked when a grown man walked into the room.

> I would not have recognized him if he had knocked me down in the street. He wasn't that same scrawny kid I had seen twenty-two years ago. I didn't say anything. I just walked over and hugged him. He hugged my back and put his face right by my ear and said, "I am so sorry I took him from you" and I said, "I know, I know."

They talked for two hours straight with intense eye-to-eye contact. George talked about prison life, his parents' divorce, and his family members. Sy talked about her family and what a bright light Zach was. After the visit, the victims' services coordinator told Sy, "I have done this job for many years and never seen anything like this before."

George and Sy now talk on the phone every week. "We tell each other all the time how much we love each other." Ron, too, has healed. "Severe hatred was killing me. I saw my wife change and thought, maybe I can, too. I feel so much love now." Ron and Sy have met George's mom, his brother, and his brother's family. His brother's daughter lived in their duplex when she got married, and Ron and Sy had dinner with them nearly every night. Both families feel that 2020 was the year of the miracle. Here is how Sy summarizes her experience:

> The difference between how I feel now and how I felt then is like night and day. It is a 180-degree opposite. I now have only love and compassion for George. He is the guy that murdered my son and he brings me so much joy. Does that make sense? Probably not, but that is how I feel. My life would not be complete without knowing him and this family. I love them so much.

* * *

Three months after coming to America, Henri Landwirth was drafted into the army. It was during the Korean War, and he thought it was a joke. But he learned that once people apply for citizenship in the United States, they are eligible to serve in the military. "Actually, I wanted to be a good citizen and didn't mind being a soldier. I felt that to be an American, you had to fight for this country."

When he left the army, he got a job at the Wellington Hotel in New York. He wanted to prove that he could succeed in America, so he did his job with tremendous passion. "I learned that the hotel business is a people business. To succeed with people, you have to give them what they want. The best way to do this is to listen, not talk."

Henri eventually moved to Florida and continued to be promoted in the hotel industry—from managing one hotel to three hotels in Cocoa Beach during the heyday of the space program. That's when he met John Glenn, the first American astronaut to orbit the earth. He and John became good friends and opened four hotels together.

One day, a wish foundation contacted Henri and asked if he would donate a room to a family they were bringing to Disney World. The young girl in the family, Amy, had incurable cancer and wanted to meet Mickey Mouse before she died. Henri was thrilled to help because he knew what it was like to be facing death every day. He could hardly wait to meet Amy and her family.

Unfortunately, the family canceled the room just before their arrival date. Amy died while the wish foundation was trying to arrange all of the free donations for the family—airline tickets, a rental car, passes to the theme parks, and so on. Henri was absolutely heartbroken. "This cannot be. How can we not fulfill a child's last wish in America?" He committed to solve this problem once and for all; his solution is Give Kids the World in Kissimmee, Florida.

Today, Give Kids the World Village has 166 villas on eighty-nine acres. It has a theater, playground, train station, fishing pond, swimming pool, town hall, chapel, and multiple restaurants. Nearly 2,000 volunteers help operate the village every week. It serves over 7,000 families each year who have a child with a terminal illness, and everything is provided for free. Since Henri launched this remarkable organization, it has welcomed nearly 200,000 families from all fifty states and seventy-six countries.

Henri Landwirth has had a lasting impact on thousands of people: the children, their families, the volunteers, the corporate sponsors, and the donors. He died in 2018 at the age of ninety-one. In my last interview with him, I asked how he was able to build such a renowned organization. Among other things, he said:

> It's ironic, but growing up in concentration camps really had a positive impact on me. Many of the survivors got sour and ended up in crazy houses because they couldn't forgive the Germans; their hate destroyed them. Other people like me have forgiven them and done something with our lives. We have the urge to be the best we can because we know life is short. My life now has new meaning. I feel wonderful getting up each morning knowing I am making a difference in the world. The problem is, I found out about it later in life. I would encourage younger people to become givers sooner. It is the way to find peace and happiness. No question!

THE APPLICATIONS

A number of forgiveness therapy programs have been developed in recent years. They all follow a similar process with specific steps for learning to let go of grudges and truly forgive others. Here are five steps I believe are the most effective and practical to implement.

1. Understand Forgiveness

Learning to forgive others starts with understanding what forgiveness is and what it is not. It is important to recognize that forgiveness does not mean

- simply telling the person he or she is forgiven,

- excusing the person for his or her actions,

- forgetting the experience ever happened,

- continuing to include the person in your life, or

- staying in an abusive or unhealthy situation.

Forgiveness is not something we do for the person who has offended us. It is something we do for ourselves, whether the other person deserves it or not. As the research suggests, holding on to anger is like drinking poison and waiting for the other person to die. Forgiveness, on the other hand, is making a conscious decision to purge the poison from our own mind and body. To truly forgive, we need to reflect on the situation, accept the reality of what happened, realize what the anger is doing to us, and decide to let go of the negative emotions so we can heal ourselves. This process takes time, effort, and commitment; it is more than just saying the words, "I forgive you."

2. Understand the Offender

I was in my office one morning when I received a call from a police officer. He asked if I had given my fiancée permission to use our business checks to buy personal items. I was confused because I had been happily married for fifteen years. It turned out this woman had broken into our office, found our box of checks, and taken a packet from the middle of the box so we would not see that the number sequence was off. She was using the checks to buy clothes around town and telling the salesclerks she was engaged to the owner of the company.

When I met with the officer, he showed me a picture of the woman and told me her story. She had a tough life, had gotten involved with the wrong crowd, and was committing petty crimes around the city. I wondered what her life had been like. Where did she grow up? How was she raised? What steps put her on this difficult path? Why did she believe committing crimes was the solution to her problems? I didn't know the answers to these questions, but I started feeling sorry for her, and my initial anger began to dissolve. We got our checkbook back, received credit for the items she had purchased, and there was little harm done. I felt genuine empathy for this woman and hoped she could resolve her problems and find greater happiness in her life.

By understanding our offenders, we are in a better position to forgive, even though it can still be difficult. As we discussed earlier, we all have an ego or self-identity that governs our thoughts, speech, and behavior. When people offend us, they are acting in accordance with their fabricated self. In other words, what they are doing makes sense to them based on their self-perceptions, even though their actions may be hurting us. If we can transcend our ego and change our behavior, people who offend us can do the same thing. Understanding who they are, why they act the way they do, and their inherent potential for change can help us develop greater empathy, compassion, and occasionally even affection for them, just as Chris Williams did for Cameron, and Ron and Sy Snarr have done for George.

3. Reflect on Positive Outcomes

None of us wants to suffer through painful experiences, and we don't want our friends or family members to suffer either. It is ironic, however, that our hardest experiences in life are often our greatest teachers—even if we don't want them to be. Henri Landwirth's experiences in five different concentration camps were horrifying, but it turned him into a person he could not have been otherwise. Here is how he summarized the outcome of his captivity:

I know what it's like to be waiting to die. This has had a big impact on what I am doing. I see a definite connection between me and the children. They have no control over their lives, and I had no control over my life in the camps. They are skinny and pale, and I see myself in their faces. This has really drawn me to them. I just want to devote my life to serving these families.

We would never want anyone to experience what Henri did, and yet he found a way to turn immense suffering into something beautiful. Although we can't always control the offenses people commit against us, we can control how we respond to these experiences. I don't want to imply that turning serious offenses into positive outcomes is easy. But when things beyond our control happen to us, we can either harbor anger and bitterness, or we can figure out how to use these experiences to improve our health and happiness. Here are some questions we can contemplate when people offend us—our answers will make it easier for us to forgive:

- Why am I feeling anger and resentment?

- What have I learned from this experience?

- What new skills or attributes can I develop?

- How can I learn greater empathy for my offender?

- How can I use this experience to help others?

4. Become a Line Etched in Water

The best way to extend forgiveness to others is to not take offense in the first place. As we develop our capacity to forgive, we transition from a line etched in stone to a line etched in the ground to a line etched in water. In this state, we don't let harsh words, disagreements, and offenses from others linger in our lives "just as a line etched in water quickly disappears and does not persist for a long time."

So how do we become a line etched in water? Buddha's concepts of "impermanence" and "nonself" offer great insights. If we recognize that all things are constantly changing and that we don't have a permanently fixed self, it is easier to not be offended by other people. In other words, the person who may offend us today will not be the same person tomorrow. Likewise, we will not be the same person tomorrow that we are today. Hence, there is no reason to be offended as we sojourn together along the path of personal development.

5. Forgive Ourselves

Finally, our ability to forgive does not become a lasting virtue until we also learn to forgive ourselves. As human beings, we all make mistakes; it is part of life. It is important to reflect on our actions, learn from our mistakes, try not to repeat them, and then let them go. When we harbor hard feelings toward ourselves, we poison our mind and body, just like we do when we hold grudges against others.

When we let our mistakes go, we purge the poison and enjoy greater health and happiness.

Forgiving ourselves is often harder than forgiving other people. The challenge is overcoming the mental chatter that accompanies offenses we commit. If we make a serious mistake or continue to repeat minor ones, our minds become megaphones of habitual thoughts: "I can't believe I did that." "I'm not as good as other people." "I can't recover from this." "I'm a real loser." These are fabricated messages being broadcast in our minds that simply aren't true. To squelch these pesky voices, some counselors prescribe a symbolic act to signal letting go once and for all. For example, we can write down the offenses that nag us and then burn the piece of paper. We can also put symbols that represent our mistakes in a box and then bury it in the ground. Next, we need to replace the false messages when they surface with true statements about ourselves, which will eventually produce more optimistic thought patterns. Here are some phrases we can repeat in our minds when the annoying voices arise:

- I am human and we all make mistakes.

- I am not the mistakes that I have made.

- I am a wonderful work in progress.

- I have learned a lot from my mistakes.

- I am stronger from correcting my errors.

- I can help people avoid similar mistakes.

- I am not the same person I was before.

In addition to managing our thoughts, doing good in the world is a powerful way to overcome our past offenses. I asked David Durocher how he got over all the harm and destruction he'd caused other people. Here is the analogy he used. Imagine our lives as an old-fashioned balance scale like the one in Figure 4-1. These were used to determine the weight of various objects. You put the object you want to weigh on one side of the scale and then add various weights on the other side until you balance the scale.

Figure 4-1: Balance Offenses with Good Deeds

In David's earlier life, he put a lot of destructive things on one side of the scale, and it was way out of balance. In order to overcome his past, he started putting good things on the other side until he balanced the scale—he said this took him nearly four years. Since then, he has put far more good things on the scale and greatly exceeded the offenses he committed in his previous life. This helped him overcome his guilt, feel good about himself, and discover a far greater happiness than he ever felt before.

In sum, the ability to forgive is an attribute we can all develop in our lives, but it takes desire, commitment, and action. As we increase our capacity to forgive, we purge a host of toxins from our mind, body, and relationships—which leads to greater happiness. Forgiveness naturally follows the first three principles in the path to happiness and civility: we dislodge our limiting ego, we refrain from judging others, and we start doing more good deeds in the world. These three principles help us build better relationships with others and make it easier to forgive when offenses occur. Now we are ready to put more good deeds on the scale by sharing what we have—our time, talents, knowledge, resources, and more—which is the next step in our path to happiness and civility.

Chapter 5

SHARE OUR GOOD FORTUNE

Rosario Lopic was born into poverty in Guatemala. She was the second-youngest of five children. Her parents both worked in the fields growing potatoes. Money for food and clothing was scarce, so Rosario learned what it was like to be hungry at a very early age.

The family only spoke Kaqchikel at home, one of the Mayan languages spoken by Indigenous people in central Guatemala; Rosario didn't speak or understand any Spanish. When she started going to school, the other kids made fun of her because her clothes were old, she had no money, and her Spanish was poor. Her classmates would all buy snacks at recess, but she never had any money to join them.

When Rosario came home from school, her parents were still working in the fields, so she and her siblings were on their own. Sometimes there was food in the cupboards and sometimes there wasn't. They waited for their parents to come home later and hoped they would bring food with them. Sometimes they did and sometimes they didn't.

One time, Rosario's parents told her she may have to quit school because they had no money, and she "cried and cried and cried." Her older sister Sabina didn't like school and agreed to drop out so their parents could use the money to pay for Rosario's education. Sabina started helping their parents and selling baskets in the marketplace to increase the family income so Rosario could stay in school. Eventually, Rosario and her younger brother were able to finish high school.

To support herself, Rosario started selling trinkets and gifts to tourists out of a small "little post" on the highway. She walked to work alone and stayed at her post all day by herself. She sold the same products as everyone else and making a living was tough. Some days, she had to sell her products at her cost, or even below her cost, in order to pay off a loan she had taken out for her inventory. Some days, she sold nothing at all. As a young single woman, walking home alone every night was terrifying because armed robbery was common on the highway. This was Rosario's life for many months.

During this difficult time, a family tragedy struck. Rosario had an older sister, Maria, who was married and had five children. Her husband was a chauffeur but barely made enough money to support their family. One night, he was tragically murdered, and the family sank to a new level of despair; the struggle to survive became much more intense for everyone. Rosario was committed to helping Maria and her children, and Sabina and her daughter. This became the driving purpose in her life.

Today, Rosario is one of the most successful businesswomen in her area. She owns a gift shop, a restaurant, a reception center, an apartment, a five-story building, and a second building she rents as office space. She has created jobs and helped support more than forty families with a total of 150 members. Many of these children are now going to school just like Rosario did. So how did she go from a life of misery to one of the happiest and most generous women in the region?

* * *

Lillia Pascual was born into poverty in Manila. She was the oldest of nine children. Her father was a fisherman, and her mother ran a small neighborhood store out of their home. Trying to provide for a large family was a huge challenge, and the children often went without adequate food and clothing.

Lillia never had the opportunity to go to school. The money was not available, and she was needed at home. When she was fifteen years old, she took a full-time job in a dress factory and became the main provider for the family. She worked extremely hard and continued to get promoted to more responsible positions. At one point, she was offered an opportunity to leave the Philippines and travel to other countries for the company. She turned down the offer because she didn't think her English was good enough for her to do the job well.

Lillia stayed with the dress company for ten years and then married when she was twenty-five years old. Her husband worked construction, and Lillia opened a small "sari-sari store" and sold a variety of goods in her neighborhood. They had four children—two boys and two girls—and struggled to make ends meet.

Over the years, her father had sold scrap lumber and Lillia saw this as a great opportunity. Many families in her area were building small homes or adding on to their homes. Since money was always a problem, used wood was an attractive solution for many of them.

Lillia started sourcing wood suppliers outside of the city, where the prices were lower. She began selling a variety of both new and used wood around Manila—bamboo, plywood, coconut, and others. Over time, coconut wood became her mainstay product. As her reputation grew as an intelligent and honest businesswoman, wood suppliers from around the region began to seek her out as a customer. She now has multiple sources for her products at excellent prices.

Lillia continued to operate her sari-sari store and worked hard to grow her wood business. Since she needed to transport her products, she also started a tricycle business. One of her tricycles is used by an employee to deliver her products, and the other is used to generate additional revenue for the family.

Today, Lillia is one of the most successful female business owners in her area. She is affectionately referred to as the "Lumber Queen of Manila." So how did she become so successful? Why is she so generous with her employees? And why is she so passionate about helping other women create thriving businesses like hers?

THE GREAT TEACHERS ON SHARING

The Hindu Sages

Acquiring possessions that we need to support ourselves and our families is noble in Hinduism. There is nothing wrong with having material things, even great wealth. The problem comes when we develop selfish attachment to these things and start believing that "we are what we own." As we discussed earlier, the Hindu sages taught that we all possess two selves in this life: a false self that develops from our earthly experiences, and a true self or atman, which is who we really are and can become. Our true self and happiness are one and the same in Hinduism.

If we become seriously attached to earthly possessions, we expand the false self, which leads to craving, greed, envy, arrogance, and bondage. When we detach from our material goods, we nurture our true self or atman, which leads to unselfishness, freedom, growth, and ultimate joy. Here are some of the great Hindu verses on wealth, attachment, and happiness.

> Never can mortals be made happy by wealth.

> One may amass wealth with hundreds of hands but one should also distribute it with thousands of hands. If someone keeps all that he accumulates for himself and does not give it to others, the hoarded wealth will eventually prove to be the cause of ruin.

Seek refuge in the attitude of detachment and you will amass the wealth of spiritual awareness.

Mahatma Gandhi may be the most revered Hindu of our modern era. Although he remained faithful to his roots, he admired Buddha, Jesus, and Muhammad and believed their teachings could be assimilated into his Hindu faith. "I prefer to retain the label of my forefathers so long as it does not cramp my growth and does not debar me from assimilating all that is good anywhere else."

Throughout his life, Gandhi was a major advocate for sharing what we have on the earth. He believed that nature provides enough for all of us as long as we don't get greedy. "There is enough in the world for everyone's need; there is not enough for everyone's greed." He revealed his lofty emphasis on detaching from material possessions when he was asked to summarize his philosophy in twenty-five words. He did it in three: "Renounce and enjoy."

Buddha

Sharing what we have is one of the noblest virtues in Buddhism. It is important for our personal development and for peace in the world. *Dana* is a word in the Pali language that means "giving," "offering," and "generosity." When Buddha taught a new group of followers, he would start with the principle of dana before teaching other moral virtues. He felt that practicing dana was a strong antidote for overcoming greed, attachment, and other human deficiencies.

What is accomplishment in generosity? Here, a noble disciple dwells at home with a mind free from the stain of miserliness, freely generous, open-handed, delighting in relinquishment, devoted to charity, delighted in giving and sharing.

Just as from a cow comes milk, from milk curd, from curd butter, from butter ghee, and from ghee comes cream-of-ghee, which is reckoned the foremost of all these, so among all households, the foremost, the best, the preeminent, the supreme, and the finest is the one who seeks wealth righteously, and shares the wealth and does meritorious deeds; and uses that wealth without being tied to it, infatuated with it, and blindly absorbed in it.

Buddha taught that sharing what we have elevates the entire community. He told this story to emphasize this principle. A king wanted to make a sacrifice that would lead to greater happiness in his life, so he asked his chaplain what he should do. The chaplain replied:

To those in the kingdom who are engaged in cultivating crops and raising cattle, distribute grain and fodder, to those in trade, give capital; to those in government service, assign proper living wages. Then those people, being intent on their own occupations, will not harm the kingdom.

The king followed the advice of his chaplain, and the result was "the king's revenues became great; the land was tranquil and not beset by thieves; and the people, with joy in their hearts, playing with their children, dwelt in open houses."

Jesus Christ

Jesus was a strong proponent of sharing what we have on this earth. He agreed with Buddha and the Hindu sages that greed, selfishness, and attachment to the things of the world are major stumbling blocks to our ultimate peace and happiness. On one occasion, he said, "It is easier for a camel to go through the eye of a needle than for a rich man to enter into the kingdom of heaven." Some biblical scholars take this literally, while others believe Jesus was referring to a small gate in the wall of the city which a camel would have trouble entering. Regardless of the interpretation, Jesus taught that loving earthly possessions inhibits our ability to experience the highest level of happiness. This is consistent with the Hindu teaching that craving material possessions expands our lesser self, while detaching from earthly goods nurtures our higher self—which is where ultimate joy is found.

Jesus also taught that true generosity requires sacrifice. A young man once asked him what he had to do to attain eternal life, and Jesus responded with a list of the commandments. When the young man said he had kept these from his youth, Jesus said, "If thou wilt be perfect, go and sell that thou hast and give to the poor, and thou shalt have treasures in heaven." On another occasion, when a poor widow placed two mites in the treasury, Jesus replied, "This poor widow hath cast more in, than all they which have cast into the treasury: for all they did cast in of their abundance; but she of her want did cast in all that she had." Although giving things we don't need is admirable, sharing things important to us leads to greater growth and happiness.

> For a man's life consisteth not in the abundance of the things which he possesseth.

> For what is a man profited if he shall gain the whole world and lose his own soul?

> For unto whomsoever much is given, of him shall be much required.

> Freely you have received, freely give.

Muhammad

Generosity is a major pillar of the Islamic faith. Muhammad taught that everything we have in life is given to us by Allah; consequently, nothing actually belongs to us. Instead, we are stewards of our possessions and need to manage them in a way that benefits the community. Two forms of giving exist in Islam. Zakat is a 2.5 percent wealth tax paid annually to care for the less fortunate. Sadaqa is voluntary giving that can take many forms—money, time, resources, advice, mentoring, and so on.

When our family lived in the Middle East, our Muslim neighbors were some of the most generous people we have known. We were constantly invited to dinners, parties, and events by our friends. When my wife Mary's brother was tragically killed, our friend Ibrahim worked tirelessly throughout the day to expedite her exit visa and get her on a plane to the United States. On another occasion, one of my students took us shopping, and his friend followed behind us and purchased the things we seemed to like.

Stories of the legendary Hatem Al Tai are often told in Islamic communities to reinforce the culture of giving. Hatem Al Tai was an extremely generous follower of Muhammad who constantly gave away everything he had. On one occasion, a royal emissary visited his home, and he killed his own prized horse so the visitor would not go to bed hungry. Hence, we often heard the saying, "He is as generous as Hatem Al Tai." Muhammad, however, was the epitome of generosity, and he encouraged his disciples to follow his example.

Competing for more distracts you until you go into your graves.

Whenever you cook some soup, add extra water and choose a family among your neighbors and give them some of it with courtesy.

Those who give, out of their own possessions, by night and by day, in private and in public, will have their reward with the Lord.

Those who are saved from their own soul's greed are truly successful.

The Philosophers

Generosity was one of Aristotle's great virtues of character. When giving of our means, he proposed a "middle way" between miserliness and wastefulness. In other words, we can acquire and enjoy our possessions, but we should freely give in appropriate ways. Not all giving is good, according to Aristotle. He argued that true generosity is giving without expectation of return and giving "to the right people, the right amounts, at the right time." Generosity should also be proportionate to our resources; those with great wealth should give more and those with modest means should give what they can. Although Confucius lived in a different era, he would have agreed with Aristotle: "Good people are generous without being wasteful; they are hardworking without being resentful; they desire without being greedy."

The teachings of Aristotle had a strong impact on Seneca. Although he was one of the richest men in Rome, he believed that material possessions were fleeting and could vanish at any time. Consequently, he would spend weeks eating simple porridges and wearing ragged clothes to detach from his wealth. This helped him understand that true happiness occurs in our minds, not in the things we own. Obsessing over material goods is like outsourcing our happiness to things that are not capable of returning genuine joy. Like Aristotle, Seneca also believed that true generosity requires us to give without expecting anything in return. "How sweet and precious is the gift given by one who won't allow any thanks, or who forgets, even as he gives, that he has given!"

THE SCIENCE ON SHARING

A new science of generosity has developed in recent years. It is an extension of the research on good deeds but focuses on our attachment to material possessions. All of us acquire lots of things during our lives: clothes, jewelry, cars, computers, tools, toys, equipment, furniture, homes, money, stocks, and so forth. Studies on generosity examine how important these things are to us, our willingness to share what we have, and the outcomes of being generous.

Possessions play a significant role in our lives, especially in our formative years. During adolescence, we want the "right" brands of shirts, pants, hats, and shoes. Owning the right car, if we can afford one, is also important. These possessions become a major part of our self-identity and signal to ourselves and others who we are, where we fit in, and what we aspire to become. As we mature into adulthood, we may become more or less attached to our possessions based on our personality, upbringing, role models, education, values, and culture. The more generous among us give things of value to other people freely and often. Unfortunately, many more of us place great value on our possessions and are less generous with other people.

The most expansive study on generosity was conducted at the University of Notre Dame as part of the Science of Generosity Initiative. The results are published in the book *The Paradox of Generosity: By Giving We Receive, but by Taking We Lose*. In this long-term study, the researchers conducted in-depth interviews across the country and collected survey data from 2,000 people. The findings from the project are clear: when we freely share what we have with other people, we are happier, healthier, suffer fewer illnesses, live with greater purpose, and experience less depression. When we cling to what we have, our possessions actually lose their value over time, we become more anxious, and we experience more depression and illnesses.

An interesting finding from this research is that generosity cannot be faked in order to achieve self-serving outcomes—just as our religious founders and philosophers taught. In other words, giving gifts grudgingly is not really giving; it won't improve our health, happiness, and relationships. To experience the positive benefits of giving, we must truly want to help other people and our community.

Hundreds of additional studies support the findings from the Science of Generosity Initiative. One fascinating body of research looks at the strength of our attachment to material possessions. "Anxious attachment" is the phrase used to describe an extreme connection to the things we own. These studies show that people with anxious attachment tend to be selfish, experience more depression, and have fewer and less satisfying relationships with people. Extreme attachment can also lead to what researchers call anthropomorphism, which is the tendency to attach human traits and emotions to our nonhuman possessions like animals, plants, cars, and other physical objects. These items often serve as substitutes for human relationships and lead to isolation, intolerance, anxiety, and ongoing distress.

The main problem with strong attachment to our possessions is they become extensions of our fabricated ego and strengthen its dominance in our lives. The stronger this egoic self becomes, the less likely we are to develop our true selves and realize our full potential. Less attachment to our possessions leads to greater introspection, purpose, growth, and happiness in our lives. Findings from the research on attachment are summarized in Table 5-1.

Table 5-1: Summary of Attachment Research

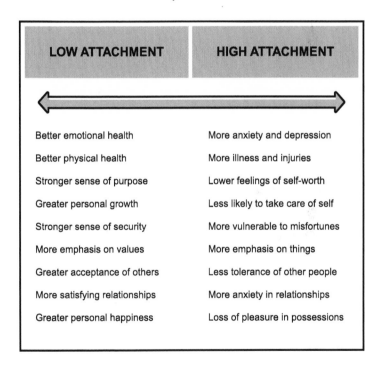

LOW ATTACHMENT	HIGH ATTACHMENT
Better emotional health	More anxiety and depression
Better physical health	More illness and injuries
Stronger sense of purpose	Lower feelings of self-worth
Greater personal growth	Less likely to take care of self
Stronger sense of security	More vulnerable to misfortunes
More emphasis on values	More emphasis on things
Greater acceptance of others	Less tolerance of other people
More satisfying relationships	More anxiety in relationships
Greater personal happiness	Loss of pleasure in possessions

Another interesting line of research has examined the causal relationship between generosity and happiness. In other words, does generosity actually increase our happiness, or are happy people simply more generous? The answer to both of these questions is yes. Happy people tend to be more generous, but generosity can also increase our happiness—even at a very early age. One study shows that toddlers exhibit greater joy when they give a treat to someone than when they get one themselves. Other studies show that happiness increases when people spend money on others, even if it's a small amount. This result occurs regardless of household income, age, gender, marital status, education, and food inadequacy. So if we become more generous, we will become happier, and as we become happier, we will become more generous. Figure 5-1 illustrates this reciprocal relationship between generosity and happiness.

Figure 5-1: Generosity and Happiness

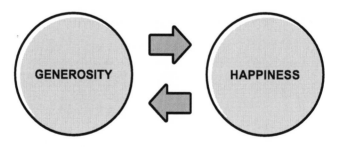

Sharing what we have has become much easier in recent years with the emergence of the new "sharing economy." This movement gives us access to many more resources without having to own them. We have online formats for sharing our cars, homes, offices, books, video games, and toys. This process is especially helpful for items we use only occasionally like tools, equipment, and recreational vehicles. We can also find people in our neighborhoods to tend our children, walk our dogs, board our pets, mow our lawns, and tutor our students. In the business world, we can find freelancers to do just about anything we need done. We can even share key employees with other companies that are not direct competitors of ours—accountants, media experts, project managers, and so on.

Jeremy Rifkin is an economic theorist, government advisor, and author of more than twenty books on technology and the economy. He argues convincingly that a third industrial revolution will usher in "a radical new sharing economy." As new technology and "smart devices" continue to automate our world, we will need more expertise in analytics, algorithms, apps, and big data management. However, there may be fewer jobs for everyone else. Consequently, Rifkin sees a future with fewer resources but far more sharing of what we have. He predicts the emergence of more social organizations, business cooperatives, and community groups that share goods, skills, knowledge, energy, and education.

This new economy will require a whole new mindset. We need to shift from a possession-oriented society to a people-oriented society. We need to think more about access to resources than ownership. We need to circulate our possessions for maximum use and keep more items out of our landfills. Ultimately, we need to nurture our basic human nature of caring and compassion for other people. This is the true revolution required in our new economy. Learning to be more generous now will prepare us for this new and better future.

I have seen the impact of generosity and sharing in my own life and in the lives of many business leaders with whom I have worked. Jon Huntsman, the benefactor of our business school at Utah State University, has been a remarkable role model. He was born into meager circumstances in Blackfoot, Idaho. His father was a music teacher, and money was scarce. As a freshman in high school, he had only one shirt, which he wore every day and washed on weekends. He also had multiple jobs and helped with the family finances. In spite of his scant upbringing, Jon committed at an early age to give away part of what he earned. When he was a young naval officer making only $300 a month, he gave away $50 each month to a family that needed it more than he did. He continued this practice throughout his entire life.

When Jon started Huntsman Chemical, he had three objectives for his earnings: (1) to pay off debt as fast as he could, (2) to upgrade equipment to make his plants safe, and (3) to donate to important humanitarian projects. In every country he did business, he would launch a social project that would benefit the people. "All businesses have a bottom line, and ours is not the building of profits. Our bottom line is the utilization of profits to enrich the human soul and to alleviate human suffering." During his life, Jon donated more than $1.5 billion to education, cancer research, poverty alleviation, religious organizations, and other causes important to him.

I have also seen many smaller-town entrepreneurs share their resources with people in their cities. Benny and Julie Benson moved to Sisters, Oregon, from Los Angeles when they grew weary of the pollution, traffic, and crime. As engineers, they started a firm that designs, builds, and operates biogas power facilities. They have now built dozens of renewable energy plants that provide power for nearly 200,000 households. They also believe that schools are the heart of any community. Consequently, they design and help teach classes at the local high school in science, technology, engineering, math, and meteorology. One of the gifts they have given the school is a brand-new biomass power plant that saves the school thousands of dollars a year on energy bills. According to Julie, "It isn't about what we do for money; it's about what we can offer the world, because engineering to me is just problem solving. It's about identifying an issue and hoping to make it better."

Gail, Will, and Gunther Williams also make significant contributions in their community. They own Idaho Sewing for Sports in Grangeville, Idaho, a company that makes padded cushions for ski lifts, schools, the military, and law enforcement. The overall purpose of their company is to create jobs and serve the people who work there. "If it is good for our employees, it is good for us." During a recent downturn in business, they had only twenty hours of work per week for each employee. Rather than lay people off, they let their employees work twenty hours each week at the company and twenty hours each week serving in the community—and everyone got paid for forty hours a week. The employees were thrilled and found numerous projects to benefit their neighborhoods: they cut wood, cleaned up yards, roofed houses, and cared for the elderly. According to Gail, "Sometimes we didn't have the money in the bank, and it would come right down to the wire, and then a job would come through the door that we could do quickly and collect the money." It was an amazing feat of generosity, and the company was able to meet payroll every week until the economy improved.

THE REST OF THE STORY

After two years of hard work, Rosario Lopic had enough cash flow to expand her business. She had a dream of what she wanted to accomplish and started making it a reality. She bought some ground and built a building. The bottom two floors are underground and became an apartment, and the ground floor became her new gift shop. After several more years, she added a fourth floor that became a restaurant, and a fifth floor that became an events center for parties, weddings, and meetings. She then built a second building she rents out as office space. "My dream was to have these things exactly as they are now—to have more customers and more services for them."

Rosario's businesses are thriving. She has paid off $260,000 in loans and now owns everything free and clear, which is unheard of for a young single woman in Guatemala. Her success has come from her passion for caring for others. "I remember what it felt like to have nothing and experience constant hardships. This has given me a desire and motivation to help people." She has provided for her sisters, her nieces and nephews, and sent one nephew to school to become a chef—he now works in her restaurant.

The way Rosario serves her community is by creating jobs and paying people well. She mentors the women who make her crafts and pays them a higher rate than other people do. She also pays her employees above-market wages, which she started doing before her loans were paid off. She has now created dozens of jobs and helped hundreds of people with various needs in her community—food, clothing, education, and mentoring. "Providing things for other people makes me feel so satisfied."

Rosario believes that sharing her possessions is necessary because they really don't belong to her. "It is very important to share what we have because nothing is ours. God is the owner of everything, and he has given me the wisdom to do what I have done." She also believes that sharing her possessions inspires other people to share what they have. She recently had a bout with cancer and was overwhelmed by the outpouring of love and kindness she received from the people she has helped. "When we are good to people, they will be good to us." Rosario's success in business and her genuine generosity have given her a life she never dreamed possible.

The greatest accomplishment in my life is what I have achieved with my business because I am able to provide work for people and help those in need. Now I can share, where before I didn't have enough money to eat. The Bible says we should love one another, and I do this by looking out for those around me. I believe all of us can be successful in life, and I gain great satisfaction from helping others better themselves. I am so happy now. There are not words to describe how I feel.

* * *

Lillia Pascual sells her wood to individuals, builders, and small neighborhood hardware stores. Hundreds of customers buy her products even though she has a number of competitors. When I asked her how she has become so successful, she replied, "People like me better than the others." She finds her customers what they want, sells them only top-quality wood, cuts it for them, and delivers it for free. She also provides snacks and treats for her customers; she has made all of them her best friends.

Lillia has five full-time employees—three are siblings, one is a relative, and one is an individual who needed work. She pays them attractive salaries plus bonuses as the business does well. She also pays for their housing, food, utilities, and other expenses, which is unheard of in her area. She is in a position to help and loves helping her team.

I know these people would help me if I needed help, so I help them. I own the company, but they help me do the work. I don't have success without them, and they don't have success without me.

Lillia now owns five homes, eight building lots, and her three businesses. Most important to her, she has put all of her children through college, and they all work in professional jobs. She feels this is her biggest accomplishment in life.

In addition to helping her family, Lillia has tremendous passion for serving her broader community. She organized a group of fifteen women who all wanted to start and operate their own business, just like she has done. Out of this group has come a manicure and pedicure business, a flower shop, a fruit stand, a clothing and shoe store, a rice cake business, several sari-sari stores, and a propane gas company.

I want to help these women do what I have been able to do. I want them to have success, security, and happiness in their lives. I really enjoy seeing them succeed. When they do well, we all do well. We all help each other to make things better for all of us.

Inspired by Lillia's example and mentoring, these women are now providing a better life for their families—they are living in nicer homes, eating better food, and sending their children to school. Lillia is especially proud of how resilient they all are when challenges arise. During the recent pandemic when many businesses in

Manila closed, all of her group members figured out ways to stay open and continue earning income. With the success of her own businesses and those of her group members, Lillia is happier than she has ever been.

> This was my dream for many years, but I never believed I could do it. I am so thankful the Lord has been so kind to me. Everything in my life has changed. Now I want to help as many people as I can. I don't want people to struggle the way that we did. I am so happy right now.

THE APPLICATIONS

1. Declutter Our Lives

Minimalist living has become popular in recent years. All you have to do is Google "How to declutter our lives," and dozens of posts, blogs, articles, and books appear. Downsizing our possessions has a number of advantages. We have fewer things to clean, organize, and store. We can reduce our debt if we are paying for things we own that we really don't need. Perhaps most important, we can devote more time to introspection, relationships, meaningful experiences, and finding new purpose in our lives.

Simply decluttering our lives, however, does not make us more generous. It's just a first step in reducing our attachment to material possessions. During this step, we are not too concerned about giving "to the right people, the right amounts, at the right time." We are simply getting rid of stuff we don't need and starting our journey of detachment from things. Here are six helpful strategies for decluttering our homes and our lives:

- **Understand That Things Don't Make Us Happy.** Lasting change always starts with a desire to be happier. Knowing that possessions are not a path to genuine joy is a first step in decluttering our lives. Although parting with our possessions can be difficult, we need to commit to do it and see what happens.

- **Start Small with One Room at a Time.** Decluttering years of possessions can be overwhelming. Once you are committed to doing it, starting small seems to work best. Start with a bathroom, then a closet, then a bedroom, then the kitchen, and finally the garage. You can do one room a week or one room a month, but just get started.

- **Create Your Decluttering Rules.** Holding emotions at bay while decluttering is critical. It helps to create rules for what goes and what stays before starting the process. For example, you might decide that anything you haven't used for six months and don't foresee using in the near future will go, and only things you use regularly will stay.

- **Make Three Piles of Things.** While sorting through your possessions, it helps to make three piles: throw away, give away, and keep for now. The throwaway pile is for things that are worthless to you and anyone else—they are simply worn out or no good. The giveaway pile is for things you don't need but others could use. The keep for now pile is only for things you use regularly.

- **Do a Serious Digital Disconnect.** Recent research shows that our "digital expressions" in social media can become part of our self-identity, in much the same way that material possessions do. Whereas former generations tended to become attached to things, our current generation may become attached to presentations of the self. Both of these reinforce our fabricated selves and interfere with who we really are and can become. Disconnecting from social media can be extremely freeing and give us more time for personal development and meaningful experiences. So try an experiment: spend thirty days disconnected from social media and see what happens.

- **Resist the Urge to Buy More.** Research shows that spending money on people, passions, and experiences results in greater happiness than buying material possessions. Every time we think about making a purchase, we should ask ourselves, "Do I really need this to meet my basic needs in life?" If not but we buy it anyway, we are adding distracting clutter to our lives.

2. Give until We Get It Right

Decluttering our lives is a first step for improving our generosity. Now it is time to go further. Three things can help us become more generous. First, we need to just start giving, even if the amount is small and our motive isn't right. Although research shows we can't fake generosity and receive positive outcomes, we are all human and have to start somewhere. Character traits take time to develop, and doing the right thing can eventually lead to the right attitude. In other words, we may need to "fake it until we make it." If we start giving small amounts consistently over time, we can eventually develop true compassion for others and a genuine love for sharing.

Second, authentic generosity grows when we give things we truly value, not things we don't want or need. For the past decade, I've had the opportunity to teach people living in poverty around the world how to start and build small businesses. I am always impressed by how generous these people become when they finally make more money, even though the amount may be small. They willingly share with their families, friends, neighbors, and the community—just like Rosario and Lillia have done. These people don't give from their surplus; they share things they need themselves. This unusual generosity leads to tremendous joy in their lives. The greater the sacrifice when sharing, the greater the happiness.

Third, generosity is enhanced when our giving involves relationships with other people. Writing checks for worthy causes and dropping off items at thrift stores are helpful ways to give, but greater happiness occurs when we get involved with those we serve. For example, Benny and Julie Benson donate to their high school, but they also teach classes to the students. Rosario and Lillia share with their families, friends, and neighbors. And Gail, Will, and Gunther Williams share their talents and resources with their local community members. Sharing with people we know builds friendships, networks, community, and better lives for everyone.

3. Try a Sharing Group

Dozens of sharing sites exist on the internet. We can find a lot of things we need for below-market rates, and some items are free or offered for trade. Sites that provide high-value products and services like transportation (Uber) and lodging (Airbnb) have become very successful. Other sites that offer smaller items like yard equipment or tools have not done as well. The main reason for this is that we're not always comfortable sharing these items with people we don't know or trust yet. Thus, it works best to form sharing groups with people we are comfortable with like family members, close friends, neighbors, book clubs, and church groups.

If you want to enhance your sharing skills, find a group of people who want to minimize their possessions and share what they have. Discuss what items you want to share, create rules for sharing, and organize a process. Sharing possessions is not easy at first, so you might want to start small with books, meals, tools, babysitting, dog walking, and so on. Group members can also share their expertise with each other—things like interior design, landscaping, investing, food storage, fitness counseling, or business advising. If things go well, you can try sharing larger and more expensive items. For example, our family members all need a truck from time to time, but we don't need five trucks. We've contributed to the cost of our son's truck so we can use it when we need it. Other items groups can share are lawnmowers, leaf blowers, tillers, power tools, a wet vacuum, a small trailer, and so on. This experiment in sharing will present some challenges, for sure. We just need to work through these and remain committed to becoming more generous and less attached to things we own.

In summary, our great religious leaders and philosophers taught that strong attachment to our possessions inhibits our personal growth and happiness. Current research confirms this principle. Attachment to possessions bolsters the artificial self, which lacks the capacity for lasting joy. In time, this leads to anxiety, depression, intolerance, poor relationships, and ironically, less pleasure in possessions. Practicing generosity strengthens the true self and leads to better health, more satisfying relationships, and greater happiness in life. Mahatma Gandhi got it right: "Renounce and enjoy."

A future economy of sharing will require a whole new mindset—one that was actually introduced thousands of years ago. This mindset will change our definitions of power and ownership and focus us on people, community, and sustainability. Kindness and doing good deeds daily will help jump-start the revolution. Detaching from our possessions and sharing what we have will follow. Now we need to identify people in our communities with specific needs that we are uniquely qualified to meet. Caring for our needy is the next principle in our path to happiness and civility.

Chapter 6

CARE FOR OUR NEEDY

Brady Murray's first son was born at ten o'clock in the morning. Although he was overcome with joy, he noticed that the doctor seemed concerned. He pulled Brady aside and told him he thought their baby had Down syndrome. "I was pretty upset and had overwhelming feelings of fear. I wasn't really sure what it meant."

As Brady stood there stunned and confused, he realized that his wife, Andrea, didn't know. When he thought about placing this burden on her right after giving birth, the darkness he was fighting grew worse. But he knelt down beside her and gave her the news. "I'll never forget how she reacted. She said, 'Great, I want to hold him. Where is he?' She didn't skip a beat and has always been okay with this; she has been very accepting and encouraging."

At one o'clock that afternoon, Brady's father came to the hospital and took him out for lunch. As they walked up to the restaurant, a couple in their sixties came out with an adult daughter who had Down syndrome. "It hit me right then…that's me! My idea of traveling the world and doing all these amazing things as a retired couple was going to change." Brady had no idea how much his life would change, and how incredibly happy he and Andrea would become because of their son Nash.

Brady knew Andrea's father, Mike, long before he met Andrea. One day, Mike invited Brady over for dinner, and he and Andrea "hit it off right from the get-go." While they were dating, they talked about their aspirations and dreams for the future. They agreed that adopting children was a great thing to do. This was the first seed planted for what was to come.

The ultimate test of their relationship came when Brady invited Andrea to a family party. "My family is crazy—aunts, uncles, cousins, and kids all over the place in my grandma's small home." Brady was nervous about how Andrea would react to the chaos. Throughout the evening, he watched as she played with the young children, helped them with their dinner, and catered to their needs. "I sensed that there was something unique about her; she had a great heart for children." This was the second seed planted for what was to come.

Today, Brady and Andrea have seven children; three of them have been adopted. Cooper is a Down syndrome child from China, and Willow and Olivia spent their first few years of life in foster care. Brady is the president of a financial organization with sixty-five full-time financial planners that service more than $1 billion in assets.

Even more significant, Brady is the founder of RODS, Racing for Orphans with Down Syndrome. He has hundreds of athletes around the country raising money during their events to help families cover the high costs of adoption. The organization has raised nearly $2 million and helped facilitate the adoption of more than sixty children with Down syndrome. So how did Brady go from a disheartened new father to the founder of an organization that blesses the lives of children with special needs and the families that adopt them?

* * *

Minnie lived in a dark and dilapidated home. She didn't mind the darkness because she was blind. She lived with her daughter who was practically catatonic from severe depression. Hunger and hopelessness were their daily existence, and they weren't sure how they were going to survive—until Rita knocked on their door.

Rita Ungaro-Schiavone went to Temple University for two years. When she got married, she left the university and "started having babies right away like most Catholics." When her children got older, she returned to school to finish her education. She planned to complete her bachelor's degree, then a master's and a PhD. But it never happened.

Rita wanted to continue volunteering while she was in school, which she had done most of her life. She went to the local YWCA and told the director she could help a half-day every week. The director gave her a list of eleven shut-ins in the community who had called and asked for assistance. Minnie was the first person she visited.

As Minnie sat on the bed with her atrophied legs dangling over the edge, Rita asked if she could get her something to drink. When she went into the kitchen, she was alarmed that there was no food in the refrigerator or cupboards. She came back with a glass of water and told Minnie, "You know, it's getting close to lunchtime and I'm hungry. How about if I get us some sandwiches?" She went to a nearby deli, picked up some lunch, and they ate together. She then asked Minnie if she could come back tomorrow and bring her a few things. "I've learned to always ask for permission to help someone." Minnie said that would be fine.

That night, Rita cooked a skillet dinner for her family with ground beef, broth, tomatoes, corn, and rice. While they were eating, she said to her husband and four sons, "This would really be good for Minnie and her daughter." So she wrapped several servings in heavy-duty foil and put them in the freezer. The next day, she went back to Minnie's home and took bed linens and the food she had cooked.

Another woman Rita visited was Dorothy. When she knocked on her door, Dorothy answered in an old winter coat that was held together with safety pins. The home was in shambles and as cold inside as it was outside. Dorothy told Rita she hadn't had heat for two weeks and was out of food. She said she was thinking about eating rat poison because she couldn't take it anymore. Rita learned that Dorothy was fifty-seven years old, her parents were dead, and a couple who befriended her had drained her bank account. Rita made arrangements to get her some heating oil and took seven frozen meals over to her house.

The meals Rita prepared for Minnie and Dorothy were some of the first of 20 million that have now been served to the elderly, homeless, and children in the greater Philadelphia area. Rita traded her dream of going back to school for a new dream: to serve as many of the homebound as possible. How did she build such a remarkable organization that meets this urgent need in her community? How has she attracted thousands of volunteers to prepare meals, deliver them, and befriend those with urgent needs in her city?

THE GREAT TEACHERS
ON CARING FOR OUR NEEDY

The Hindu Sages

Life was difficult during the time of the Hindu sages. Many people were hunters and gatherers, spending much of their time searching for food. Consequently, caring for the poor and hungry was an important principle taught by these sages. If you were fortunate enough to have any kind of wealth, you should share it with the needy because you may require their assistance in the future. This cycle of good fortune and misfortune was believed to be a normal part of life. Thus, caring for the poor benefited everyone in the community.

> Refuse not food to those who are hungry. When you feed the hungry, you serve the Lord, from whom is born every living creature.

Bounteous is he who gives unto the beggar who comes to him in want of food and feeble. Success attends him in the shout of battle. He makes a friend of him in future troubles.

Let the rich satisfy the poor implorer, and bend his eye upon a longer pathway. Riches come now to one, now to another, and like the wheel of carts are ever rolling.

Buddha

Buddha discovered the vast amount of suffering in the world during his first foray outside the walls of his palace. From that time forward, his entire life was devoted to alleviating human suffering. One of the ways we can do this is to give desirable gifts to the poor in our communities. Buddha emphasized ten specific items we can give to the needy: food, drink, clothes, transportation, garlands, perfumes, medicines, beds, lighting, and dwelling places. Those willing to share these gifts will enjoy many desirable gifts in return.

> Monks, if people knew, as I know, the result of giving and sharing, they would not eat without having given, nor would they allow the stain of miserliness to obsess them and take root in their minds. Even if it were their last morsel, their last mouthful, they would not eat without having shared it if there were someone to share it with.
>
> A noble female disciple, by giving food, gives four things to the recipient. What four? By giving long life, she herself will be endowed with long

life, human or divine. By giving beauty, she herself with be endowed with beauty, human or divine. By giving happiness, she herself will be endowed with happiness, human or divine. By giving strength, she herself with be endowed with strength, human or divine.

Jesus Christ

In Christianity, God is the father of our spirits and we are all brothers and sisters on this earth. Just as any parent hopes other people will help their children who are suffering, God wants us to care for our brothers and sisters who are suffering. The words *serve, servant,* and *service* are mentioned hundreds of times in the Bible. In the four gospels alone, Christ refers to the poor dozens of times. To experience the greatest joy in this life and the life hereafter, we are encouraged to feed the hungry, clothe the naked, care for the sick, and visit the incarcerated.

They that be whole need not a physician, but they that are sick.

He that hath two coats let him impart to him that hath none, and he that hath meat, let him do likewise.

When thou makest a dinner or a supper, call not thy friends, nor thy brethren, neither thy kinsmen, nor thy rich neighbors; lest they also bid thee again, and a recompence be made thee. But when thou makest a feast, call the poor, the maimed, the lame, the blind: And thou shall be blessed; for they cannot recompense thee.

Insomuch as ye have done it unto one of the least of these my brethren, ye have done it unto me.

Muhammad

Caring for the needy was a major teaching of the Prophet Muhammad. He was particularly concerned about the hungry, the sick, the elderly, orphans, and slaves. He taught that caring for the needy would bring great joy into our own lives and compensate for mistakes we have made.

Feed the hungry, visit the sick, and set captives free.

The one who visits the sick is in an orchard of paradise.

Be merciful to the orphan, stroke his or her head gently with feelings of love and compassion and feed him with your food. Your heart will become soft, and you will be successful in what you do.

If you give charity openly, it is good, but if you keep it secret and give to the needy in private, that is better for you, and it will atone for some of your bad deeds.

According to Muhammad, caring for the needy benefits the entire community. In one particular hadith, he tells the story of people drawing lots for seats on a boat. Some get excellent seats in the upper deck, and some get poor seats in the lower deck. Those in the upper deck have water, but those in the lower deck do not.

People in the lower deck have to continually walk up to the upper deck to get water, which angers the privileged passengers there. After a while, a man in the lower deck starts cutting a hole in the boat to get water for his thirsty companions. Those in the upper deck have a decision to make. If they let the man continue cutting the hole, the boat will sink and they will all perish. If they freely share their water, they will all be saved. Here is the moral of the story: To have a civil society, the rich and the poor need to work together for the benefit of everyone in the community.

The Philosophers

Caring for the poor made political sense to Aristotle. He felt that a strong middle class was the key to a well-functioning society. If we have only rich and poor people, disaster will constantly loom at the gate—just as Muhammad expressed in his analogy of the upper and lower decks on the boat. Members of a larger middle class are perfect mediators between the rich and poor. Since they generally want to improve their own lives, they don't hate or punish the rich. On the other hand, they have tremendous compassion for the poor because many of them have come from this class, which gives the poor hope that they too can improve their lives. Hence, Aristotle's emphasis on caring for the poor was an effort to create a more civil society.

Aquinas was influenced by Aristotle, but his emphasis on the poor was more compassionate than functional. He felt the best way to show our love for God was to love and care for the needy in our communities. When we care for our needy, we are essentially emulating God's love and goodness to us. Aquinas believed we should care for the needy who are closest to us first—family, friends, neighbors—and then care for those with the greatest needs in our broader community.

Cicero believed there are two ways to help the needy. First, we can give them money, and second, we can give them "personal service." He believed the second approach was superior to the first. If we give people money, there is no mentoring or ongoing support, and in the long run, we are able to help fewer people as our money runs out. If we give people our time and support, we have greater capacity, and those we help may follow our example and become givers themselves. Thus, Cicero believed that providing service to those in need is the best way to cultivate peace and civility in our communities.

THE SCIENCE ON CARING FOR OUR NEEDY

Caring for our needy is the sixth principle in our path to happiness and civility. It closely follows doing good deeds and sharing our good fortune. Doing good deeds daily involves looking for opportunities to be kind and helpful to those around us. We might visit an ailing family member, help a neighbor with a project, volunteer at a school, or carry an elderly person's groceries. Sharing our good fortunate involves detaching from our material possessions, which feed and reinforce our fabricated ego. The things we own do not have the ability to produce a deep and lasting joy.

Caring for our needy goes one step further. It focuses on the urgent needs of those who are suffering or marginalized in our communities. Helping these people obviously improves their lives, but it also benefits the givers of the service and the entire community, just as our great teachers and philosophers taught thousands of years ago. Let's first review how caring for our needy improves their lives and our communities. Then we will discuss how caring for our needy benefits those who serve them.

Although Cicero argued that giving people money was not as helpful as providing personal service, research shows that giving money to the poor can improve both their lives and the community. In a study in Kenya, 10,500 families in 653 rural villages were each given $1,000 US dollars. This amount was approximately three-quarters of their regular annual income and a 15 percent increase in total income for the region. These families used this money to improve their circumstances—they bought more food, better food, clothing, shelter, and sent their children to school. Equally important, they purchased these products and services from providers in the community, which improved these businesses. After eighteen months, it was determined that each dollar donated led to $2.70 in increased economic activity in the region. Although giving money to the poor may not be sustainable in the long run, it is a good start to improving their lives.

Other studies show the benefits of Cicero's second approach for helping the needy—offering personal service. An interesting study shows that our attitudes toward the poor—and the way we talk to them—make a difference in how well they respond to our assistance. Viewing them as the "poor," "needy," "disadvantaged," "underprivileged," "high risk," and so on does not motivate them to improve their lives. In fact, it cultivates an attitude of entitlement that devalues their potential for growth. On the other hand, cultivating a "horizontal view" of relationships—that we all have value—and being positive, encouraging, and empowering produces the best results. A great deal of evidence suggests that training, education, friendship, and ongoing mentoring are the most powerful catalysts for change.

We have seen this occur in our SEED poverty alleviation program. We have taught thousands of people around the world and helped them start and develop successful small businesses. An initial loan helps them get started, but the ongoing mentoring, encouragement, following up on goals, and helping them find resources is what produces long-term success. We continue to mentor people for months and even years if they need our help. We have seen hundreds of families who were earning $200 a month double, triple, and even quadruple their household income. Ongoing personal service makes the difference.

Caring for our poor and needy produces many positive outcomes in their lives: the hungry are fed, the lonely gain friendship, the sick become well, the homeless are sheltered, and the unlearned are educated. But what happens to the givers of the service? One extensive study shows that if we buy something for someone in need, we are happier than when we buy something for ourselves. This research has been duplicated in 120 countries worldwide with the same results regardless of the income, education, race, and ethnicity of the givers. The good feeling that comes from helping someone in need appears to be universal. In addition to greater happiness, numerous studies show that caring for people in need produces many of the same outcomes we enjoy from doing good deeds daily and sharing our good fortune:

- lower levels of stress, anxiety, and depression

- lower blood pressure and fewer illnesses

- greater longevity and life satisfaction

- a greater sense of purpose and belonging

- more positive relationships in our lives

In order to experience these benefits, research shows that we have to develop a personal value for caring. If we have empathy for the poor but don't feel a responsibility to help, we generally don't do anything. In addition, we have to serve the needy for the right reasons —because we truly care about them and want to help improve their lives and our community. As Seneca taught, serving others to get something in return is only a loan, a self-centered act that doesn't increase our happiness.

I have seen the positive outcomes of caring for those with urgent needs on numerous occasions. Reverend Jay and Toni Ragsdale are the founders of Fill the Pot Ministry in Salt Lake City and two of the most generous people I know. When Jay's brother became homeless and was living in a piano box, Jay drove all the way from California to Salt Lake to help him through his crisis. Later, Jay became homeless, and his brother took him in and helped him get back on his feet.

The two brothers became ordained ministers and committed to help people who were struggling the way they had been. Unfortunately, their plans came to a halt when Jay's brother died of a heart attack. Jay decided to continue the ministry on his own in honor of his brother, and he and his wife, Toni, went to work. They started feeding people every Sunday morning who were camped in Pioneer Park, the same place where Jay's brother had lived in a piano box. It started with 10 people, then 35, then 135, and then 400–600 every Sunday.

> The early days were tough. We had really rough winters and really hot summers. We would load and unload the trailer no matter what the weather. We were like the mailman—we would deliver no matter what.

After eleven years, the city let them use an old warehouse across the street from the park. Today, they feed hundreds of people every Sunday morning—for many, it is the only nutritious meal they get each week. According to Jay, three types of people show up: (1) the career homeless, (2) the mentally ill, and (3) people who have fallen on hard times—they have lost a job, gone through a divorce, had a major medical problem, or are working but don't make enough money to pay rent.

Hundreds of individuals, schools, churches, and community organizations donate food, funding, cook the meals, and serve the guests. Fill the Pot Ministry also provides clothing, bins for personal items, Alcoholics Anonymous classes, career education, and résumé writing. It all works because hundreds of community members have become as passionate about helping the homeless as the Ragsdales are.

> We may have started this, but it is not our ministry. All the people that come here, it is their ministry. We are all working together and giving back to the community. Many people who come here were on one side of the line to start with, and now they are on the other side of the line serving. We change each other as we go through this world together.

Fill the Pot Ministry has significantly changed the lives of Reverend Jay and Toni. They have a strong sense of purpose, they feel they have value, they have made dozens of incredible friends, and they are happier than they have ever been. Yet, Jay looks forward to the day when Fill the Pot Ministry will no longer be needed.

I always say the greatest day will be when there are only two people left in this building—just me and Jesus. Then we can smile because we'll know that everybody has been taken care of.

I have also seen a remarkable transformation occur with the students who participate in our SEED poverty alleviation program. They spend one semester studying entrepreneurship and small business consulting and then spend a full semester somewhere in the world teaching people who are struggling to climb out of poverty. I hear two general themes from these students when they return to the United States. "I feel like I have hit the lottery in life" and "I want to be a generous giver for the rest of my life." Here's how a few of them describe the increased joy they now experience from serving those in need.

I can honestly say this program is life changing. I went out with the intent of helping other people, determined to change their lives for the better. Through working with them, getting to know them, and a million hugs from little old women asking us where we have been their whole life, it was my life that was changed.

I am a new person because of this experience. Few things have helped me grow and feel as fulfilled as I do in my life.

Seeing the strength, love, and positivity of the Filipino culture taught me more about friendship, charity, and gratitude than I'd ever learned elsewhere, and I can't be more grateful for that.

Living in Peru and working with the people there has changed me forever.

I have established many amazing friendships through this program that have helped me become a better person and live a more fulfilled and happy life. Being able to provide a "hand up" instead of a "hand out" to those in need was easily one of the greatest experiences I've had, one that I will never ever forget.

THE REST OF THE STORY

Brady Murray started learning all he could about Down syndrome: health challenges, mental capacity, life expectancy, and so on. He learned that children with Down syndrome are very friendly, compassionate, nonjudgmental, and they like to make people happy. Nash turned out to be a great gift to the family and the entire community.

I love to take Nash places and observe people when they see him. They immediately become their best self—more patient, more kind, more loving, more encouraging—because that's the way Nash is. When we are around someone who is kind, patient, and loving, we become kind, patient, and loving. I call it their superpower; they bring out the best in people, no question. That is why we adopted another child with Down syndrome. We wanted to double down on that positive influence in our family and the community.

Even though these children bring great joy into people's lives, babies with Down syndrome in many countries are put in orphanages at birth and transferred to adult mental institutions at the age of five. Most of them live unhappy lives and die an early death. Brady learned that many families want to adopt these special children, but the cost is prohibitive—$30,000–$40,000 for an international adoption. Brady felt he could help with this problem. "It's one thing to go to people and ask them to adopt a child with Down syndrome from across the world, but if there are people ready to do it and it's a financial matter, we could raise money."

During this time, Brady decided he wanted to participate in triathlons to stay in shape. So he did his first half-triathlon, which is 70.3 miles: a 1.2-mile swim, a 56-mile bike ride, and a 13.1-mile run. It was a total disaster. "I was literally half-dead and I didn't know if I would ever be able to walk again." A while later, he tried it again with the same result. He felt that he could never do a full triathlon and decided to hang up his running shoes. But Andrea reminded him that he always dreamed of completing a full Ironman and suggested he use the event to raise awareness and funds for children with Down syndrome. Brady knew he couldn't do it for himself but felt that he could do it for these children.

> I completely changed my paradigm and got caught up in a cause that wasn't about me; it was about saving kids. All of a sudden, my mindset, training, and everything shifted, and I became a triathlete. When we get caught up in causes that are bigger than ourselves, we witness miracles. The way to get caught up is by focusing on others.

Andrea was completely supportive of Brady's madness: 40 miles of running every week, 200 miles of biking, 10,000 meters of swimming. He was on his bike at 4:00 a.m., swimming at 5:00 a.m., and then out running. He successfully completed his first full Ironman and raised thousands of dollars for the adoption of several children with Down syndrome.

Brady next set his sights on the Ironman World Championship in Kona, Hawaii. You have to qualify to get into Kona and only the best athletes in the world participate. That particular year, however, the organizers opened up eight spots for people with inspiring stories to tell. Brady was one of the eight selected from 105 applications. He was off to Hawaii to share the RODS story.

Kona was extremely difficult. The 2.4-mile swim went okay, and the bike was fine for eighty miles, but the last thirty-two miles were excruciatingly painful. When Brady got off his bike, his legs were completely trashed. He thought about walking but knew he had to finish for the kids. The pain never stopped, but he plodded onward. Finally, at twenty-four miles, he knew he would finish. When he crossed the finish line, he hugged Andrea like he had "never hugged her before." Then he got a big surprise: the Ironman organization had a $20,000 check waiting for him in addition to the thousands of dollars he had raised himself.

With nearly $2 million raised by hundreds of athletes to place more than sixty orphans in great homes, RODS is still running strong.

Here is how Brady summarizes his experience:

> I have had people ask me, "If you could make it so Nash didn't have Down syndrome, would you?" The first day, the first week, the first month, I probably would have wanted that. Looking at it now, there is no way! That is his gift, that is his superpower. I wouldn't change that for the world. Our goal now is to inspire more families to answer the call and give these children the opportunity to use their superpower. I know from experience that families that answer the call are going to be the ones that benefit the most.

• • •

Rita Ungaro-Schiavone was totally committed to her new mission. She felt strongly that no one should be hungry or lonely in a world of caring people. She just needed to put a system in place to make this happen. She first went to her parishioners at Saint Jerome's Church and told them what she wanted to do. They agreed that each family would cook an extra portion of their dinner each night, put it in an aluminum TV tray, and place it in their freezer. Once a week, volunteers would pick up the frozen dinners and take them to a central freezer. Additional volunteers would then take seven meals to an elderly shut-in once each week and visit for an hour. The program was a big hit with the congregation.

Before long, other religious leaders asked Rita to share her program with their congregations. She was shocked when a Lutheran pastor asked her to give a sermon in her church. At the time, Catholic women did not stand at the altar and preach sermons, particularly to members of another faith. This led to a flood of offers to speak at other churches and on radio shows. Before long, Rita had more than 200 churches and synagogues duplicating her program around Philadelphia.

Within a few years, Aid for Friends had hundreds of freezers in all five counties of the city, thousands of volunteers, and was feeding thousands of elderly shut-ins every week. Here is how the program worked: About half of the meals came from individuals and families who made extra portions of their dinners. The other half came from churches, synagogues, schools, and other groups that cooked multiple meals at a time. Saint Ignatius Church, for example, provided 12,000 meals in one year alone. Volunteers then took these meals to the elderly and developed friendships with them.

Rita introduced a simple yet remarkable solution to a major problem we have in all of our cities. It utilizes food that is normally wasted and distributes it to people who need it the most. Each year in America, approximately 80 billion pounds of food are wasted. This is more than 200 pounds per person and nearly 40 percent of our total food supply each year. In addition to reducing food waste, the program allows thousands of volunteers to each make a difference in the life of one person in their city. It is the "one brick" that Arshay Cooper suggests we each pick up to build an amazing bridge we can all cross.

Unfortunately, Rita died a few years ago at the age of eighty-two. Her amazing organization continues to thrive on the strong foundation she built. In 2019, the name was changed to Caring for Friends to reflect the broader mission of the organization. Skilled leaders continue to provide needed services throughout the five counties in Philadelphia. Today, Caring for Friends has more than 10,000 volunteers, serves nearly 30,000 individuals, and has delivered more than 20 million meals. What a difference a passionate woman, with the help of thousands of others, has made in the world.

It's funny how things work out. I traded my dream of going back to school for a new dream: to serve as many of the homebound as possible. These are people nobody cares about, including some of their families. But we can be their friends. My motto is "Food and friendship: little miracles love can bring."

THE APPLICATIONS

1. Choose One

We all know people who need our help or assistance. We may be uniquely qualified to help some of these people based on our relationship, contacts, experiences, education, or training. We don't need to start an organization like Brady and Rita have done, but we can all help at least one person and make a huge difference in his or her life. As Reverend Jay Ragsdale always says, "If one person helps one person who helps one person, the world would be in a lot better shape."

When we sincerely contemplate who we can help—whether through meditation, prayer, reflection, or research—I believe we get a clear answer. It is a basic principle of life that works for people who want to make a difference in the world. So here's an experiment you can try. Make a list of people you know who need some type of assistance—it can be financial, mentoring, friendship, training, or problem solving—and contemplate who on the list you are best positioned to help based on your resources and experiences. Follow the impressions you get and start helping. I am confident you will be a great gift to that person, and helping him or her will be a great gift back to you. All you have to do is try it and see what happens.

2. Present Options

Jennie Taylor was on a weekend getaway with her girlfriends when she got the phone call. Two soldiers had just shown up at her home and told her mother they had to talk to Jennie in person. She had already had a very traumatic year—everything that could happen to humble a person had already happened: her husband, Brent, had been deployed in Afghanistan for more than ten months; she was home alone with their seven children; their house flooded and they had to live in a rental condo for seven months; she was adjusting to their first teenager; and she was nursing their young baby. Jennie's weekend getaway was the break she needed to recover from all these things.

When her mom called that morning, Jennie thought something had gone wrong with one of the children. Instead, her mom said, "There are two army officers at the door, and they say they need to talk to you and only you." They agreed to meet at a National Guard office that was halfway between her home and where she was staying with her friends. That's when she got the news that her husband, Brent, had been killed in Afghanistan.

Since Brent was the mayor of their city, hundreds of people knew him and wanted to help. During this time, Jennie learned what was most helpful for her family in the wake of this traumatic ordeal. She gives great advice on how we can help people who are suffering with pain, grief, trauma, or depression.

> It was very helpful when people gave me options. Someone might say, "What can we do for you?" or "What do you need?" I had no idea. I didn't know how to answer, and it was very overwhelming. What helped the most was when people would say, "Would it be more helpful if I did your laundry or took the kids for a couple of hours?" In the thick of pain, trauma, or grief, things are so overwhelming. When you give me choices, I don't feel like I am completely incapable— I kind of need you to think for me. So if you don't know what to do for a person in crisis, imagine you are in that crisis and make a list, pick a couple of things, and ask which one might be helpful.

Even if you are just taking dinner to a family, you can say, "Would you prefer pot roast and mashed potatoes or pasta primavera?"

Or you can say, "I have three hours to help tomorrow. I can mow and trim your lawn or run errands for you. Which would be most helpful?" Giving people choices makes it easier for them early on, and it gets the process of helping started. As time goes on, you may be able to create a plan together that will be the most helpful to them in the long run.

3. Support a Cause

In Chapter 3, "Do Good Deeds Daily," we talked about joining an organization that needs volunteers and encouraged you to find opportunities to serve in your community. When we commit to worthy causes, we are more likely to do good deeds on a regular basis. So supporting an organization that someone else has started is a good idea.

Many organizations need volunteers to usher at sporting events, teach community classes, raise money for the arts, support environmental causes, and so on. Other organizations work directly with the poor and needy in our communities. Although working one-on-one with someone in need is the greatest contribution we can make, working with an organization that serves the needy allows us to strengthen our communities further. If the time is right for additional service in our lives, we can benefit many individuals and our communities.

4. Accept Help When Needed

Many of us are more comfortable helping others than we are receiving help. Maybe we are too proud, embarrassed, or just don't want to bother people with our own challenges. Being willing to accept help, however, is critical to completing the full development of human relationships. We have to both give and receive to grow closer to people. This is what Arshay Cooper did when his team assumed the role of teachers and helped the Chicago police officers develop rowing skills—and it significantly improved their relationships.

Years ago, I was working as an advisor to a group of college students. I was helping them with school, careers, dating, health issues, and so on. I grew weary of this role at times, and it wasn't always as rewarding as I had hoped it would be. Then I skied off a cliff and broke my back. I had a six-hour surgery in the middle of the night that fused five vertebrae with metal rods and cadaver bone. Suddenly, these students were showing up at my door to cheer me up and provide meals for our family. Since students don't always cook, it was usually fast food—pizzas, hamburgers, Chinese, and so on—but our kids loved it! This experience completed the cycle of caring for me, and I developed much more enjoyable relationships with these students.

The help we need may be simple advice, friendship, training on a subject, or meals during a difficult time. Letting people help us when they offer is vital for strengthening our relationships; sometimes we will give, and sometimes we will receive. As the Hindu sages taught, *riches come now to one, now to another, and like the wheel of carts are ever rolling.*

In summary, the poor and needy in our communities often lack the basic essentials of life. Consequently, they are more inclined to suffer from emotional and physical conditions like anxiety, depression, hopelessness, heart disease, stroke, cancer, and diabetes. These conditions impact all of us in our communities. When we care for the poor and needy, we make life better for everyone—the receiver, the giver, and the community. When we help the sick, we develop compassion. When we serve the poor, we cultivate gratitude. When we share our resources, we realize we have value. In the process, we build a community that is caring, compassionate, healthy, and joyful—we become one people and one planet!

CONCLUSION

Implementing Your Happiness Plan

I have a number of heroes in my life. Keith and Verla Curtis are two of my favorites—they are my wife, Mary's, parents. They married young and struggled to make ends meet following the Great Depression. After six years of marriage, Keith was drafted into the army on December 24, 1943; he was twenty-nine years old, and they had a child. Apparently, there were not enough younger men in his draft region, so they kept moving up the age range until they filled the quota for the area. It didn't matter that he was nearly thirty years old, married, and had a family. Keith and Verla had just built a new home, but Verla and their daughter couldn't afford to stay there on a private's salary, so they moved in with her parents and rented out their home.

Keith was assigned to the 29th Infantry Division and sent to Camp Wheeler in Georgia for training. After six months of "learning how to kill in order to stay alive," he landed on Omaha Beach in July 1944 as one of the replacement soldiers following the D-Day invasion. The fighting began the day he arrived.

We were lying along a hedgerow, about ten feet between each man. The man ahead of me and the man in back of me were both killed. From that day in July until late October in 1944, I lived under battle conditions almost every day, seeing men get blown to pieces under these awful combat conditions. I would go for two or three weeks at a time without having an opportunity to take off my shoes and socks. My clothes were filthy dirty, but there was no chance to clean up.

Keith was wounded in one of these battles and given a Purple Heart, but he stayed in the field and continued fighting. After three months of brutal combat, an officer walked through their camp, calling Keith's name. He was told the general wanted to see him at headquarters. Since he was older, had a college degree, and could type, he was asked to serve as the general's assistant for the rest of the war. In this role, he ended up typing the death certificates for almost every man in his platoon. The only time he ever mentioned the war to Mary was when she complained about a typing class. He responded, "You need to learn to type; it saved my life." If he hadn't learned to type, Mary wouldn't be here, and I wouldn't be married to this amazing woman.

Prior to the war, Keith had a job at the Utah Railroad Company; he returned to that job after the war. Forty-two years later, he retired as the president of the company. After his death, Verla came to live at our home for four years. It was a remarkable experience and our kids loved her. She was happy, positive, and never said a negative word about anyone or anything. Even though she was in her nine-ties, she would get out of bed every morning, fall to her knees, and thank God for all the great things in her life. She would then plan one thing to do that day for someone else—a phone call, a visit, a meal, or a gift of money. Little did I know that she was teaching me three important therapies for healing ourselves and increasing our happiness. I call them thought therapy, talk therapy, and action therapy. Here is how they work.

Thought Therapy

A few years ago, Mary and I, our son Jay, and our business partner, Shawn, rode our bikes across America. We started on the Pacific Ocean in the small town of Florence, Oregon, and finished on the Atlantic Ocean in Yorktown, Virginia. To complete this 4,000-mile journey in the time we had allotted, we needed to average nearly one hundred miles every day. We quickly realized that how we thought made all the difference in this crazy world we had created for ourselves. Instead of thinking, "My legs are fried. I don't know how I can possibly ride another hundred miles today," we started thinking, "Sure, my legs are tired, but I can do this. I'll slow down if I need to and maybe take a longer lunch break." So we quit asking each other, "How are you feeling today?" and started asking, "How are you thinking today?" Our escapade became more enjoyable every day, and when we finished our ride in Yorktown, we all felt we could turn around and ride our bikes back to the West Coast, no problem.

The important lesson: We feel the way we think. This is what Viktor Frankl discovered as a prisoner in four concentration camps during World War II. As a psychiatrist, he was fascinated by who lived and who died in the camps. It wasn't the biggest and strongest physically who lived but those who remained positive about the future and found some meaning in their suffering. Frankl concluded that our mind is the last great frontier of freedom, and although we cannot control all of our circumstances, we can control how we think about and react to them. This is exactly what Verla did through all the challenges she faced. She hit her knees first thing in the morning and focused on what was good, positive, and meaningful in her life—we feel the way we think.

Talk Therapy

Whereas thought therapy is how we talk to ourselves, talk therapy is how we talk to each other. In Chapter 2, we discussed how our communication creates our reality. Remember the two old guys from *Sesame Street*? Every experience, event, situation, and person has both positive and negative attributes. The way we talk about them frames our reality and impacts our thought processes. It's like holding an empty picture frame up to the world during our conversations and sliding it back and forth along a continuum of positive and negative attributes. Once we anchor the frame through our communication, that particular worldview becomes solidified.

I have found that people who are generally negative about life feel that positive people are simple and naive, that they are living in a bubble that isn't reality. I would argue that the positive aspects of experiences, situations, and people are just as real as the negative attributes. We just need to decide which world we want to live in, and positive communication produces a more joyful life. Verla was also a great example of this. Mary told me she never heard her mom make a negative or derogatory comment about anyone or anything during her entire life.

Action Therapy

The dramatic changes that occurred in David Durocher's life resulted from him "acting as if." He acted as if he were honest, and he eventually became honest. He acted as though he had compassion, and he eventually became compassionate. He acted as though he were a decent person, and he eventually became a decent person. Prolonged action over time impacts both our thoughts and our talk and becomes an integrated and authentic part of our character. So the way to become a better person is to act the way better people act.

When we become discouraged, unhappy, or depressed, we tend to act based on how we feel, which is understandable. If we don't feel good, we may skip a class, dinner, party, or event. As hard as it may be, we need to continue acting if we want to become happier and experience more joy in our life. This is how John Brewer handles being paralyzed:

It's kind of like riding a bike uphill, you have to keep pedaling, you have to keep working on it, gravity is always there. When I get discouraged, I have to be still and think about what truly makes me happy, and then I decide who could use a shout-out or help from me that day.

This is what Verla did throughout her life—she acted. Mary has many memories of tagging along with her as she made visits, delivered food, and cleaned houses.

These three therapies support and reinforce each other as depicted in Figure C-1. We can start at any point in the cycle to bring our thoughts, talk, and actions into harmony. For example, changing our thinking can influence our talk and our actions. Likewise, changing our talk can influence our actions and our thinking. And changing our actions can influence our thinking and our talk.

Figure C-1: Thought, Talk, and Action

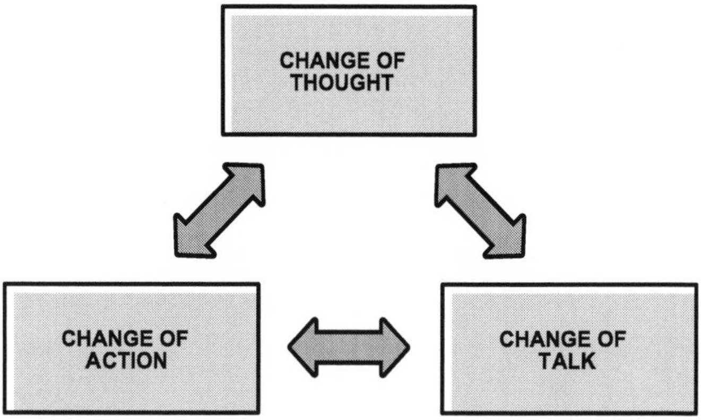

This notion of uniting our thoughts, talk, and actions is not new. During his life, Mahatma Gandhi is reported to have said, "Happiness is when what you think, what you say, and what you do are in harmony." His point is significant: when our thoughts, words, and actions are consistently aligned, we experience greater harmony, peace, and happiness in our lives.

So how can we apply these three therapies to cultivate the six principles of happiness and civility in our lives? The key is to start changing our thoughts, talk, and actions regarding each principle. As a brief review, let's discuss the six universal truths in light of the three therapies for change.

Give Up the Ego

Understanding that our ego or self-identity is a fabrication of our experiences in life, particularly during our younger years, can start the process of change. We can now entertain more positive thoughts about who we are and have the potential to become. As our thoughts become more optimistic, our conversations will become more positive. There is no reason to make degrading comments about our skills, looks, intelligence, talent, or opportunities when talking with others. In addition, as we discussed in Chapter 1, taking small action steps outside of our comfort zone will enhance our self-perceptions. Table C-1 lists some of the thoughts, talk, and actions we might consider in order to develop a healthier and more positive self-identity.

Table C-1: Give Up the Ego

GIVE UP THE EGO
ENHANCING THOUGHTS
My self-perceptions are not who I really am.
I am not superior or inferior to anyone else.
I have potential to do great things in my life.
ENHANCING TALK
I have a way to go but I am making progress.
I haven't done that before but I am willing to try.
My success is largely due to support from others.
ENHANCING ACTIONS
Take a course at the local community college.
Develop some new skills to help your career.
Sign up and train for a community fitness event.

Refrain from Judging

Once we realize that our self-perceptions have come from a host of experiences in our lives and are not who we really are or could become, it is easier to understand that our perceptions of other people are probably inaccurate and incomplete as well. This should stimulate new thinking about people who are different from us and lead to more positive conversations about them. Also, befriending and getting to know people from different backgrounds, races, cultures, and religions will help eliminate our biases. Table C-2 summarizes the thoughts, talk, and actions we can take to reduce our tendency to judge other people.

Table C-2: Refrain from Judging

REFRAIN FROM JUDGING
ENHANCING THOUGHTS
We are all equal upon this earth.
My perceptions of others are not always accurate.
We are more alike than we are different.
ENHANCING TALK
I think she has a lot of good qualities.
If we talk to him it will probably help.
I need to get to know them better.
ENHANCING ACTIONS
Visit the worship services of various religions.
Volunteer at a food bank or homeless shelter.
Learn the language and culture of another country.

Do Good Deeds Daily

When we obsess about ourselves, we bring a full range of human emotions into our lives: fear, worry, anxiety, discouragement, and depression. When we think more about other people, we stop our self-centered ruminations and cultivate concern, understanding, and compassion in our lives. So doing good deeds daily starts with shifting our thinking from ourselves to other people and how we might help them. As our thoughts change, our conversations will also shift from "It's all about me" to "How are others doing today?" Of course, taking action is the ultimate key to developing this practice of doing good deeds daily. Table C-3 lists some ideas for aligning our thoughts, talk, and actions around this important principle of joyful living.

Table C-3: Do Good Deeds Daily

DO GOOD DEEDS DAILY
ENHANCING THOUGHTS
I want to do something for someone today.
Is there anyone I know who may need my help?
I will look for opportunities to contribute today.
ENHANCING TALK
How are things going for you today?
Is there anything I can do for you?
Let's see if we can help this new family.
ENHANCING ACTIONS
Take a welcome gift to a new family.
Mentor a student who needs your expertise.
Call and visit with a friend or relative.

Forgive One Another

As human beings, we are going to offend and be offended by others —it's part of the human experience. Holding on to grudges, however, can be a poison in our lives that limits our inner peace and happiness. We need to accept this fact in our thoughts and acknowledge it in our conversations with others. Knowing that we are all evolving will help us let go of hard feelings and forgive people when offenses do occur. The ultimate goal is to not take offense in the first place. Table C-4 summarizes some thoughts, talk, and actions we can take to nurture the principle of forgiveness in our lives.

Table C-4: Forgive One Another

FORGIVE ONE ANOTHER
ENHANCING THOUGHTS
Am I holding grudges against anyone?
What can I do to make this situation right?
I want to let go of these negative feelings.
ENHANCING TALK
She is still learning and can overcome this behavior.
I don't think he's actually aware of what he is doing.
I know he can change this behavior in the future.
ENHANCING ACTIONS
Forgive a former friend who has hurt your feelings.
Forgive a colleague or boss who has offended you.
Forgive yourself for a past mistake you have made.

Share Our Good Fortune

Material things don't have the potential to make us truly happy in life. In fact, obsessing about them can bring us a great deal of anxiety, fear, lust, and disappointment. When we choose to share what we have, however, we become happier, healthier, suffer fewer illnesses, and experience less depression. Understanding this principle and talking about it with others are important steps in becoming more generous. But like all of these universal principles, we have to take action to experience the full benefits of sharing. Table C-5 summarizes some of the thoughts, talk, and actions we can take to develop this attribute.

Table C-5: Share Our Good Fortune

SHARE OUR GOOD FORTUNE
ENHANCING THOUGHTS
I have all the basic things I need in my life. Material things don't provide true happiness. Sharing what I have will produce a deeper joy.
ENHANCING TALK
I am happy to share what I have with others. What are some of the things these people need? I am happy to contribute to this worthy cause.
ENHANCING ACTIONS
Declutter your life one room at a time. Keep sharing until it becomes more natural. Start a sharing group with friends or family.

Care for Our Needy

Caring for those in need in our communities benefits all of us. Accepting this fact starts the change process, and talking with other people about it spreads the message. Most importantly, we need to choose people we are uniquely qualified to help based on our personal experiences and resources, and find ways to help improve their lives, which improves ours in the process. Table C-6 lists some thoughts, talk, and actions we can take to better care for our needy and strengthen our communities.

Table C-6: Care for Our Needy

CARE FOR OUR NEEDY
ENHANCING THOUGHTS
I have a lot to give and want to help others.
I have time to mentor or help someone in need.
I would like to help make our community stronger.
ENHANCING TALK
If we work together we can solve this issue.
I am willing to do my part to improve our city.
I am happy to teach these students this skill.
ENHANCING ACTIONS
Help someone prepare a résumé and find a job.
Mentor a student from a high-risk environment.
Prepare meals for a family that is struggling.

ONE PEOPLE ONE PLANET

On July 8, 1776, a 2,000-pound bell rang from the tower of the Pennsylvania State House. It was summoning citizens to the first public reading of the Declaration of Independence, which had been approved by members of the Continental Congress four days earlier. No loftier document has ever been written about a people's desire for freedom and self-government. It boldly declares that all people have certain unalienable rights that cannot be taken from them and that governments exist to protect these rights.

One of the rights Thomas Jefferson included in the Declaration of Independence was "the pursuit of happiness," a new political doctrine at the time. Jefferson borrowed this concept from the English philosopher John Locke, who borrowed it from the Greek philosophers Aristotle and Epicurus. According to Locke, there is "imaginary happiness" and "real happiness." Imaginary happiness comes from actions that produce short-term pleasure but long-term misery. Real happiness comes from pursuing principles and actions that lead to an everlasting joy. Locke argued that pursuing "true and solid happiness" is the foundation of liberty and can lead to the best possible life for human beings and the greatest good for society.

The majestic language of the Declaration of Independence sent the hearts of the people soaring and gave them a vision for a better world. This vision allowed this small band of freedom lovers to defeat the most powerful military in the world. It also inspired them to work together to create strong communities: they built each other's homes and barns; they planted and harvested each other's crops; they planned their schools, roads, and businesses; and they cared for the sick and afflicted among them. It was a magnificent display of "all for one and one for all."

Leaders from around the world watched this experiment in freedom with great curiosity. The ruling nobles hoped it would fail; their citizens hoped it would succeed and set a new precedent in the world. A French political philosopher named Alexis de Tocqueville came to America in 1831 to observe this bold experiment up close for nearly a year. He believed the magic of this new form of self-government happened in the small townships.

> When an American needs the assistance of his fellows, it is very rare for that to be refused, and I have often seen it given spontaneously and eagerly. When there is an accident on the public road, people hurry from all sides to help the victim. When some unexpected disaster strikes a family, a thousand strangers willingly open their purses, and small but very numerous gifts relieve their distress. It often happens in the most civilized countries in the world that a man in misfortune is almost as isolated in the crowd as a savage in the woods. That is hardly ever seen in the United States.

Although Tocqueville was extremely impressed with the collaboration among these new settlers, he was very concerned that the unalienable rights that were supposed to apply to everyone were offered to some groups and not to others, which is inconsistent with the philosophy of a free society. He was particularly concerned about the institution of slavery and the treatment of the original inhabitants of this continent. He felt that inequality among the races was the greatest threat to this grand experiment in freedom and feared it would fail. After returning to France, he remarked, "I hope to see the day when the law will grant equal civil liberty to all the inhabitants of the same empire, as God accords the freedom of the will, without distinction, to the dwellers upon earth."

Here we are, nearly 200 years after Tocqueville's visit to America, and I wonder what he would think of our society today. Our cities are much larger and far more populated. We no longer need each other's physical labor and have forfeited the emotional bonds it once created. We can live next to our neighbors for years and never get to know them or understand their challenges. Loneliness, discouragement, depression, intolerance, discrimination, civil unrest, and hatred between political parties seem to be the norm.

The good news is, we have a path that can make things better for everyone if we choose to follow it. The six universal principles presented in this book can help all of us find the "true and solid happiness" described by Locke and build the kinds of civil communities observed by Tocqueville. These proven principles were introduced thousands of years ago by our great religious founders and philosophers and more recently supported by research in positive psychology. This merging of ancient wisdom with modern science is the solution for including everyone, improving our relationships, strengthening our communities, and healing our nations.

Here is a vision I have for our future. What if every community across the country formed a One People One Planet civic group that included citizens from our diverse backgrounds, races, ethnicities, religions, sexual orientations, and socioeconomic statuses? What if these groups were to meet each month to discuss critical issues facing their communities? And what if these groups also planned and implemented regular projects to solve the critical issues they face, just like the small townships did at the time of Tocqueville?

Engaging in respectful conversations to learn more about each other and then working side by side on important issues will help us focus on shared values, see that we are more alike than we are different, overcome our biases, and eventually create a One People One Planet culture. This inclusive culture will be a positive influence on other families, neighborhoods, and communities. I think this is a goal worth working toward. How about you?

REFERENCES

Introduction: Our Quest for Happiness

Kaneda, Toshiko, and Carl Haub. "How Many People Have Ever Lived on Earth." Population Reference Bureau. May 18, 2021. https://www.prb.org/howmany peoplehaveeverlivedonearth/.

"List of Religious Populations." Wikipedia. Last edited March 13, 2022. https://en.wikipedia.org/wiki/List_of_religious_populations.

The Editors of Encyclopedia Britannica. "Marsilio Ficino." *Encyclopedia Britannica*. October 15, 2021. https://www.britannica.com/biography/Marsilio-Ficino.

"Perennial Philosophy." Wikipedia. Last edited March 15, 2022. https://en.wikipedia.org/wiki/Perennial_philosophy.

Huxley, Aldous. *The Perennial Philosophy: An Interpretation of the Great Mystics, East and West*. New York: Harper Perennial Classics, 2012.

Al Taher, Reham. "The 5 Founding Fathers and a History of Positive Psychology." PositivePsychology.com. November 25, 2021. https://positivepsychology.com/founding-fathers/.

Brahma, Apuruseya, and A. B. Keith. *The Four Vedas: Translated in English*. Translated by R. T. Griffith and M. Bloomfield. N. p.: Hindu E-Press, 2018.

Dharma, Krishna. *Mahabharata: The Greatest Spiritual Epic of All Time*. N.p.: Krishna Dharma Publisher, 2008.

Easwaran, Eknath. *The Bhagavad Gita*. Tomales, CA: Nilgiri Press, 2007.

Easwaran, Eknath. *The Upanishads*. Tomales, CA: Nilgiri Press, 2007.

Bodhi, Bhikkhu. *In the Buddha's Words: An Anthology of Discourses from the Pali Canon*. Somerville, MA: Wisdom Publications, 2005.

Bodhi, Bhikkhu. *The Buddha's Teachings on Social and Communal Harmony: An Anthology of Discourses from the Pali Canon*. Somerville, MA: Wisdom Publications, 2016.

Byrom, Thomas. *The Dhammapada: The Sayings of the Buddha*. New York: Vintage Books, 2011.

Bercholz, Samuel, and Sherab Chodzin Kohn. *The Buddha and His Teachings*. Boulder, CO: Shambhala, 1993.

Hanh, Thich Nhat. *The Heart of Buddha's Teachings*. New York: Harmony Books, 2015.

McManners, John. *The Oxford Illustrated History of Christianity*. New York: Oxford University Press, 2001.

The Holy Bible: King James Version, 1611 Edition. Peabody, MA: Hendrickson Publishers, 2010.

The Qur'an. Translated by M. A. S. Abdel Haleem. New York: Oxford University Press, 2016.

Ondigo, Yahya M. *Forty Hadiths on Good Moral Values*. Riyadh, Saudi Arabia: International Islamic Publishing House, 2010.

The Analects of Confucius: A Philosophical Translation. Translated by Roger T. Ames and Henry Rosemont Jr. New York: Ballantine Books, 1999.

"Teachings of Confucius." http://confucius-1.com/teachings/.

Duignan, Brian. "Philosophers to Know, Part I." *Encyclopedia Britannica*. Accessed March 22, 2022. https://www.britannica.com/list/philosophers-to-know-part-i.

"Socrates." *Stanford Encyclopedia of Philosophy*. Revised February 8, 2018. https://plato.stanford.edu/entries/socrates/.

"Plato." *Stanford Encyclopedia of Philosophy*. Revised February 12, 2022. https://plato.stanford.edu/entries/plato/.

"List of Manuscripts of Plato's Dialogues." Wikipedia. Last edited March 7, 2022. https://en.wikipedia.org/wiki/List_of_manuscripts_of_Plato%27s_dialogues.

"Aristotle." *Stanford Encyclopedia of Philosophy*. Revised August 25, 2020. https://plato. stanford.edu/entries/aristotle/.

Seneca, Lucius Annaeus. *Letters from a Stoic*. London, England: Penguin Books, 1969.

Seneca, Lucius Annaeus. *On the Happy Life*. Translated by Roger L'Estrange. N.p.: n.p., 2020.

Cicero, Marcus Tullius. *On Duties*. Translated by Walter Miller. Moscow, ID: Roman Roads Media, 2016.

Chenu, Marie-Dominique. "St. Thomas Aquinas." *Encyclopedia Britannica*. March 3, 2022. https://www.britannica.com/biography/Saint-Thomas-Aquinas.

"John Locke." Pursuit of Happiness. Accessed March 22, 2022. https://www.pursuit-of-happiness.org/history-of-happiness/john-locke/.

"Genetics vs. Genomics Fact Sheet." National Human Genome Research. Last updated September 7, 2018. https://www.genome.gov/about-genomics/fact-sheets/Genetics-vs-Genomics.

Chapter 1: Give Up the Ego

Personal conversations with David Durocher.

Personal conversations with Salsa Queen Zapata.

Easwaran, Eknath. *The Upanishads*. Tomales, CA: Nilgiri Press, 2007.

Shiah, Yung-Jong. "From Self to Nonself: The Nonself Theory." *Frontiers in Psychology*. February 4, 2016. www.frontiersin.org/articles/10.3389/fpsyg. 2016.00124/full.

Bercholz, Samuel, and Sherab Chodzin Kohn. *The Buddha and His Teachings*. Boulder, CO: Shambhala, 1993.

The Holy Bible: King James Version, 1611 Edition. Peabody, MA: Hendrickson Publishers, 2010.

The Qur'an. Translated by M. A. S. Abdel Haleem. New York: Oxford University Press, 2016.

Abdullah, Amatullah. "Prophet Muhammad's Last Sermon: A Final Admonition." IslamReligion.com. Last modified October 18, 2015. https://www.islam religion.com/articles/523/prophet-muhammad-last-sermon/.

McKay, Brett, and Kate McKay. "What Is a Man? The Allegory of the Chariot." Last updated September 25, 2021. https://www.artofmanliness.com/character/manly-lessons/what-is-a-man-the-allegory-of-the-chariot/.

Leary, Mark. "What Is the Ego, and Why Is It So Involved in My Life?" *Psychology Today*, May 2019. https://www.psychologytoday.com/us/blog/toward-less-egoic-world/201905/what-is-the-ego-and-why-is-it-so-involved-in-my-life.

Mehrad, Aida. "Mini Literature Review of Self-Concept." *Journal of Educational Health and Community Psychology* 5, no. 2 (August 2016): 62–66. https://www.researchgate.net/publication/315101634_Mini_Literature_Review_of_Self-Concept.

Escalas, Jennifer. "Self-Identity and Consumer Behavior." *Journal of Consumer Research* (Winter 2012). https://academic.oup.com/jcr/pages/self_identity_and_consumer_behavior.

Carfora, V., D. Caso, and M. Conner. "The Role of Self-Identity in Predicting Fruit and Vegetable Intake." *Appetite* 106, no. 1 (November 2016): 23–29. https://www.sciencedirect.com/science/article/abs/pii/S019566631530129X?casa_token=fczazSOjD4cAAAAA:tjHR9Y_bVq3_s2gucfBGir7ENosHo ADIAOCZIc_MhrPtBsA5bW7v-v_Ou_I93376hCj-smS6YA.

Feinstein, Brian, Rachel Hershenberg, Vickie Bhatia, and Jessica A. Latack. "Negative Social Comparison on Facebook and Depressive Symptoms: Rumination as a Mechanism." *Psychology of Popular Media Culture* 2, no. 3 (July 2013): 161–70. https://www.researchgate.net/publication/259997458_Negative_social_comparison_on_Facebook_and_depressive_symptoms_Rumination_as_a_mechanism.

Vogel. Erin A., Jason P. Rose, Bradley M. Okdie, Katheryn Eckles, and Brittany Franz. "Who Compares and Despairs? The Effect of Social Comparison

Orientation on Social Media Use and its Outcomes." *Personality and Individual Differences* (June 2015). https://static1.squarespace.com/static/576b2868bebafbdcb747da7c/t/581bf3b5b3db2bd19dfcd552/1478226870231/2015_Okdie_PAIDb.pd.

Wayment, Heidi A., and Jack J. Bauer, eds. *Transcending Self-Interest: Psychological Explorations of the Quiet Ego*. Washington, DC: American Psychological Association, 2008.

Wayment, Heidi A., Jack J. Bauer, and Kateryna Sylaska. "The Quiet Ego Scale: Measuring the Compassionate Self-Identity." *Journal of Happiness Studies* 16 (2015): 999–1033. https://link.springer.com/article/10.1007/s10902-014-9546-z.

Eva, Nathan, Mulyadi Robin, Sen Sendjava, Dirk van Dierendonck, and Robert C. Liden. "Servant Leadership: A Systematic Review and Call for Future Research." *The Leadership Quarterly* 30, no. 1 (February 2019): 111–32. https://www.sciencedirect.com/science/article/pii/S1048984317307774#!.

Saleem, Farida, Yingying Zhang, C. Gopinath, and Ahmad Adeel. "Impact of Servant Leadership on Performance: The Mediating Role of Affective and Cognitive Trust." *Sage Open* (January 2020). https://doi.org/10.1177/2158244019900562.

LePera, Nicole. "How to Do Ego Work." YouTube. November 25, 2019. https://www.youtube.com/watch?v=OSz-BKKTbBE.

Chapter 2: Refrain from Judging

Personal conversations with Chalon Keller, daughter of Dora Gay Martin, and correspondence with her siblings Holly Keller Perkins and Tim Keller

Personal conversations with Arshay Cooper.

Cooper, Arshay. *A Most Beautiful Thing*. New York: Flatiron Books, 2020.

Easwaran, Eknath. *The Upanishads*. Tomales, CA: Nilgiri Press, 2007.

Wood, Ernest, and S. V. Subrahmanyam. *The Garuda Purana*. N.p.: n.p., 2021.

Bodhi, Bhikkhu. *In the Buddha's Words: An Anthology of Discourses from the Pali Canon.* Somerville, MA: Wisdom Publications, 2005.

Borg, Marcus, ed. *Jesus and Buddha: The Parallel Sayings.* Berkeley, CA: Ulysses Press, 2004.

Byrom, Thomas. *The Dhammapada: The Sayings of the Buddha.* New York: Vintage Books, 2011.

Gier, Nick. "The Buddha on Judgement and Acceptance." *The Reader,* May 2016. https://sandpointreader.com/the-buddha-on-judgement-and-acceptance/.

The Holy Bible: King James Version, 1611 Edition. Peabody, MA: Hendrickson Publishers, 2010.

The Qur'an. Translated by M. A. S. Abdel Haleem. New York: Oxford University Press, 2016

Ondigo, Yahya M. *Forty Hadiths on Good Moral Values.* Riyadh, Saudi Arabia: International Islamic Publishing House, 2010.

Mayer, John D. "Why Confucius Had No Time to Judge." *Psychology Today,* March 2009. https://www.psychologytoday.com/us/blog/the-personality-analyst/200903/why-confucius-had-no-time-judge.

Gambardella, Steven. "Seneca: Curbing Snobbery: A Little Humility Goes a Long Way." *The Sophist,* June 2019. https://medium.com/the-sophist/seneca-curbing-snobbery-b686ae87ed12.

Plato. *The Republic of Plato.* Translated by Allan Bloom. New York: Basic Books, 2016.

"Understanding Unconscious Bias." NPR, July 15, 2020. https://www.npr.org/2020/07/14/891140598/understanding-unconscious-bias.

"The Ultimate List of Cognitive Biases: Why Humans Make Irrational Decisions." HumanHow. http://humanhow.com/list-of-cognitive-biases-with-examples/.

"An Interactive Literature Review Table on Implicit Bias 2019." Kamm Solutions. https://kammsolutions.com/wp-content/uploads/2019/08/Kamm-Solutions-Implicit-Bias-Lit.-Review-Table-.pdf.

Kirwan Institute for the Study of Race and Ethnicity, The Ohio State University. "State of the Science: Implicit Bias Review 2017." http://kirwaninstitute.osu. edu/implicit-bias-training/resources/2017-implicit-bias-review.pdf.

Maruyama, Hana. "Teachers Give Higher Grades to More Attractive Students." *Education Week*, January 2014. https://www.edweek.org/leadership/study-teachers-give-higher-grades-to-more-attractive-students/2014/01.

Shpancer, Noam. "Poor Predictors: Job Interviews Are Useless and Unfair." *Psychology Today*, August 31, 2020. https://www.psychologytoday.com/us/ blog/insight-therapy/202008/poor-predictors-job-interviews-are-useless-and-unfair.

Sullivan, Bob, and Hugh Thompson. "Now Hear This! Most People Stink at Listening." *Scientific American*, May 3, 2013. https://www.scientificamerican. com/article/plateau-effect-digital-gadget-distraction-attention/.

Chapter 3: Do Good Deeds Daily

Personal conversations with John Brewer.

Personal conversations with Lola Strong.

Easwaran, Eknath. *The Bhagavad Gita*. Tomales, CA: Nilgiri Press, 2007.

Easwaran, Eknath. *The Upanishads*. Tomales, CA: Nilgiri Press, 2007.

Bodhi, Bhikkhu. *The Buddha's Teachings on Social and Communal Harmony: An Anthology of Discourses from the Pali Canon*. Somerville, MA: Wisdom Publications, 2016.

Byrom, Thomas. *The Dhammapada: The Sayings of the Buddha*. New York: Vintage Books, 2011.

Bercholz, Samuel, and Sherab Chodzin Kohn. *The Buddha and His Teachings*. Boulder, CO: Shambhala, 1993.

The Holy Bible: King James Version, 1611 Edition. Peabody, MA: Hendrickson Publishers, 2010.

The Qur'an. Translated by M. A. S. Abdel Haleem. New York: Oxford University Press, 2016.

Ondigo, Yahya M. *Forty Hadiths on Good Moral Values*. Riyadh, Saudi Arabia: International Islamic Publishing House, 2010.

Seneca, Lucius Annaeus. *How to Give: An Ancient Guide to Giving and Receiving*. Princeton, NJ: Princeton University Press, 2020.

Aristotle. *The Nicomachean Ethics*. New York: Penguin Classics, 2004.

Floyd, Shawn. "Thomas Aquinas: Moral Philosophy." Internet Encyclopedia of Philosophy. https://iep.utm.edu/aq-moral/.

Stefon, Matt. "Ren Chinese Philosophy." *Encyclopedia Britannica*. Accessed March 22, 2022. https://www.britannica.com/topic/ren.

Siegel, Steve. "The Art of Kindness." Mayo Clinic Health Systems. May 29, 2020. https://www.mayoclinichealthsystem.org/hometown-health/speaking-of-health/the-art-of-kindness.

Local Government and Communities Directorate. "Volunteering for All: National Framework—Literature Review." Scottish Government. April 25, 2019. https://www.gov.scot/publications/literature-review-scotlands-volunteering-outcomes-framework/pages/6/.

Davis, Jeanie Lerche. "The Science of Good Deeds: The 'Helper's High' Could Help You Live a Longer, Healthier Life." WebMD. https://www.webmd.com/balance/features/science-good-deeds#1.

Curry, Oliver Scott, Lee A. Rowland, Caspar J. Van Lissa, Sally Zlotowitz, John McAlaney, and Harvey Whitehouse. "Happy to Help? A Systematic Review and Meta-analysis of the Effects of Performing Acts of Kindness on the Well-Being of the Actor." *Journal of Experimental Social Psychology* 76 (May 2018): 320–29. https://www.sciencedirect.com/science/article/pii/S0022103117303451.

Office of Research and Policy Development. "The Health Benefits of Volunteering: A Review of Recent Research." Corporation for National and Community Service. April 2007. https://americorps.gov/sites/default/files/evidenceexchange/FR_2007_TheHealthBenefitsofVolunteering_1.pdf.

Schreier, Hannah M. C., Kimberly A. Schonert-Reichl, and Edith Chen. "Effect of Volunteering on Risk Factors for Cardiovascular Disease in Adolescents: A Randomized Controlled Trial." *JAMA Pediatrics* 167, no. 4 (April 2013): 327–32. https://jamanetwork.com/journals/jamapediatrics/fullarticle/1655500.

Moll, Jorge, Frank Kruegger, Roland Zahn, Matteo Pardini, Ricardo de Oliveira-Souza, and Jordan Grafman. "Human Fronto–mesolimbic Networks Guide Decisions about Charitable Donation." *Proceedings of the National Academy of Science* 103, no. 42 (October 2006): 15623–28. https://www.pnas.org/content/103/42/15623.

Evans, Richard Paul. "How I Saved My Marriage." RichardPaulEvans.com. February 9, 2015. https://www.richardpaulevans.com/2015/02/09/saved-marriage/.

"Tanganyika Laughter Epidemic." Wikipedia. Last edited March 17, 2022. https://en.wikipedia.org/wiki/Tanganyika_laughter_epidemic.

Chapter 4: Forgive One Another

Personal conversations with Ron and Sy Snarr.

Personal conversations with Henri Landwirth. The full story first appeared in my book *The Business of Heart: How Everyday Americans Are Changing the World.* Salt Lake City: Shadow Mountain Publishing, 1999.

Dharma, Krishna. *Mahabharata: The Greatest Spiritual Epic of All Time.* N.p.: Krishna Dharma Publisher, 2008.

Bodhi, Bhikkhu. *The Buddha's Teachings on Social and Communal Harmony: An Anthology of Discourses from the Pali Canon.* Somerville, MA: Wisdom Publications, 2016.

The Holy Bible: King James Version, 1611 Edition. Peabody, MA: Hendrickson Publishers, 2010.

The Qur'an. Translated by M. A. S. Abdel Haleem. New York: Oxford University Press, 2016.

Ondigo, Yahya M. *Forty Hadiths on Good Moral Values*. Riyadh, Saudi Arabia: International Islamic Publishing House, 2010.

Aristotle. *The Nicomachean Ethics*. New York: Penguin Classics, 2004.

Brown, Montague. "St. Thomas Aquinas on Human and Divine Forgiveness." *The Saint Anselm Journal* 6, no. 2 (Spring 2009). https://www.anselm.edu/sites/default/files/Documents/Institute%20of%20SA%20Studies/4.5.3.1_62Brown.pdf.

Essential Confucius. Translated by Thomas Cleary. Los Angeles: Castle Publishing, 2000.

The Analects of Confucius: A Philosophical Translation. Translated by Roger T. Ames and Henry Rosemont Jr. New York: Ballantine Books, 1999.

Weir, Kirsten. "Forgiveness Can Improve Mental and Physical Health." CE Corner, American Psychological Association 48, no. 1 (January 2017). https://www.apa.org/monitor/2017/01/ce-corner.

"Forgiveness: Your Health Depends on It." Johns Hopkins Medicine. Accessed March 23, 2022. https://www.hopkinsmedicine.org/health/wellness-and-prevention/forgiveness-your-health-depends-on-it.

"Forgiveness Research." International Forgiveness Institute. Accessed March 23, 2022. https://internationalforgiveness.com/research/.

Enright, Robert. "Reflecting on 30 Years of Forgiveness Science." *Psychology Today*, April 2019. https://www.psychologytoday.com/us/blog/the-forgiving-life/201904/reflecting-30-years-forgiveness-science.

Williams, Chris. *Let It Go*. Salt Lake City: Shadow Mountain Publishing, 2012.

Chapter 5: Share Our Good Fortune

Interviews with Rosario Lopic, translated from Spanish by Andy Thunell.

Interviews with Lillia Pascual, translated from Tagalog by Jaren Hunsaker.

Brahma, Apuruseya, and A. B. Keith. *The Four Vedas: Translated in English*. Translated by R. T. Griffith and M. Bloomfield. N. p.: Hindu E-Press, 2018.

Easwaran, Eknath. *The Bhagavad Gita*. Tomales, CA: Nilgiri Press, 2007.

Easwaran, Eknath. *The Upanishads*. Tomales, CA: Nilgiri Press, 2007.

Ajai, R., and Shakuntala A. Singh. "Gandhi on Religion, Faith and Conversion: Secular Blueprint Relevant Today." *Mens San Monographs* 2, no. 1 (January 2004): 79–88. https://www.ncbi.nlm.nih.gov/pmc/articles/PMC3400300/.

Patel, Nehal A. "Renounce and Enjoy: The Pursuit of Happiness through Gandhi's Simple Living and High Thinking." *Seattle Journal for Social Justice* 13, no. 2 (2014). https://digitalcommons.law.seattleu.edu/cgi/viewcontent. cgi?article=1746&context=sjsj.

Bodhi, Bhikkhu. *The Buddha's Teachings on Social and Communal Harmony: An Anthology of Discourses from the Pali Canon*. Somerville, MA: Wisdom Publications, 2016.

The Holy Bible: King James Version, 1611 Edition. Peabody, MA: Hendrickson Publishers, 2010.

The Qur'an. Translated by M. A. S. Abdel Haleem. New York: Oxford University Press, 2016.

Ondigo, Yahya M. *Forty Hadiths on Good Moral Values*. Riyadh, Saudi Arabia: International Islamic Publishing House, 2010.

Aristotle. *The Nicomachean Ethics*. New York: Penguin Classics, 2004.

Behrents, Rolf G. "Aristotle on Generosity." *American Journal of Orthodontics and Dentofacial Orthopedics* 151 (2017): 831–32. https://www.ajodo.org/article/ S0889-5406(17)30244-5/pdf.

The Analects of Confucius: A Philosophical Translation. Translated by Roger T. Ames and Henry Rosemont Jr. New York: Ballantine Books, 1999.

Gambardella, Steven. "Seneca: Curbing Snobbery: A Little Humility Goes a Long Way." *The Sophist*, June 28, 2019. https://medium.com/the-sophist/ seneca-curbing-snobbery-b686ae87ed12.

Seneca, Lucius Annaeus. *On the Happy Life*. Translated by Roger L'Estrange. N.p.: n.p., 2020.

Smith, Christian, and Hilary Davidson. *The Paradox of Generosity: Giving We Receive, Grasping We Lose.* New York: Oxford University Press, 2014.

Allen, Summer. "The Science of Generosity." Greater Good Science Center, UC Berkeley. May 2018. https://ggsc.berkeley.edu/images/uploads/GGSC-JTF_White_Paper-Generosity-FINAL.pdf.

Cafasso, Jacquelyn. "What Is Anxious Attachment?" *Healthline*, November 14, 2019. https://www.healthline.com/health/mental-health/anxious-attachment.

Norberg, Melissa M., Cassandra Crone, Cathy Kwok, and Jessica R. Grisham. "Anxious Attachment and Excessive Acquisition: The Mediating Roles of Anthropomorphism and Distress Intolerance." *Journal of Behavioral Addictions* 7, no. 1 (March 2018): 171–80. https://www.ncbi.nlm.nih.gov/pmc/articles/PMC6035017/.

Aknin, Lara B., J. Kiley Hamlin, and Elizabeth W. Dunn. "Giving Leads to Happiness in Young Children." American Psychological Association. June 2012. https://journals.plos.org/plosone/article?id=10.1371/journal.pone.0039211.

American Psychological Association. "In Rich and Poor Nations, Giving Makes People Feel Better than Getting, Research Finds." 2013. https://www.apa.org/news/press/releases/2013/02/people-giving.

Sundararajan, Arun. *The Sharing Economy: The End of Employment and the Rise of Crowd-Based Capitalism.* Boston: MIT Press, 2016.

Rifkin, Jeremy. "The Third Industrial Revolution: A Radical New Sharing Economy." YouTube. 2018. https://www.youtube.com/watch?v=QX3M8Ka9vUA.

Davis, Paul M. "Survey Finds Trust Is #1 Barrier to Sharing." Shareable. July 10, 2012. https://www.shareable.net/survey-finds-trust-is-1-barrier-to-sharing/.

Chapter 6: Care for Our Needy

Personal conversations with Brady Murray.

Personal conversations with Rita Ungaro-Schiavone. The full story first appeared in my book *The Business of Heart: How Everyday Americans Are Changing the World* (Salt Lake City: Shadow Mountain Publishing, 1999).

Brahma, Apuruseya, and A. B. Keith. *The Four Vedas: Translated in English.* Translated by R. T. Griffith and M. Bloomfield. N. p.: Hindu E-Press, 2018.

Easwaran, Eknath. *The Upanishads.* Tomales, CA: Nilgiri Press, 2007.

Bodhi, Bhikkhu. *The Buddha's Teachings on Social and Communal Harmony: An Anthology of Discourses from the Pali Canon.* Somerville, MA: Wisdom Publications, 2016.

The Holy Bible: King James Version, 1611 Edition. Peabody, MA: Hendrickson Publishers, 2010.

The Qur'an. Translated by M. A. S. Abdel Haleem. New York: Oxford University Press, 2016.

Ondigo, Yahya M. *Forty Hadiths on Good Moral Values.* Riyadh, Saudi Arabia: International Islamic Publishing House, 2010.

Charles. "Why Inequality Matters: Aristotle and the Middle Class." Underground Network. March 2016. https://underground.net/aristotle-and-the-middle-class/.

"What Is Generosity?" Science of Generosity Project, University of Notre Dame. Accessed March 23, 2022. https://generosityresearch.nd.edu/more-about-the-initiative/what-is-generosity/.

Cicero, Marcus Tullius. *On Duties.* Translated by Walter Miller. Moscow, ID: Roman Roads Media, 2016.

Egger, Dennis, Johannes Haushofer, Edward Miguel, Paul Niehaus, and Michael Walker. "General Equilibrium Effects of Cash Transfers: Experimental Evidence from Kenya." December 18, 2019. http://emiguel.econ.berkeley.edu/wordpress/wp-content/uploads/2021/03/GE-Paper_2019-12-18.pdf.

Crawford, Krysten. "'Poverty Alleviation' and 'Needy'? Why Words Can Do More Harm than Good When Offering Help, Stanford Study Finds." *Stanford News,* June 25, 2020. https://news.stanford.edu/2020/06/25/poverty-alleviation-needy-words-can-harm-good-offering-help/.

American Psychological Association. "In Rich and Poor Nations, Giving Makes People Feel Better than Getting, Research Finds." 2013. https://www.apa.org/news/press/releases/2013/02/people-giving.

Bekkers, René, and Mark Ottoni-Wilhelm. "Principle of Care and Giving to Help People in Need." *European Journal of Personality* 30, no. 3 (May 2016): 240–57. https://www.ncbi.nlm.nih.gov/pmc/articles/PMC5111750/.

Personal conversations with Reverend Jay and Toni Ragsdale.

Multiple conversations with SEED international interns from Utah State University.

Personal conversations with and public presentations by Jennie Taylor.

Conclusion: Implementing Your Plan

Personal journal of Keith Curtis.

Glauser, Michael. *Main Street Entrepreneur: Build Your Dream Company Doing What You Love Where You Live.* Irvine, CA: Entrepreneur Press, 2016.

Frankl, Viktor E. *Man's Search for Meaning.* New York: Washington Square Press, 1985.

Personal conversations with John Brewer.

Morrissey, Mary. "What Gandhi Wants You to Know about the Power of Positive Thinking." HuffPost, December 6, 2017. https://www.huffpost.com/entry/what-gandhi-wants-you-to-know-about-the-power-of-positive-thinking_b_10487524.

Glauser, Michael. *The Business of Heart: How Everyday Americans Are Changing the World.* Salt Lake City: Shadow Mountain Publishing, 1999.

"John Locke." Pursuit of Happiness. https://www.pursuit-of-happiness.org/history-of-happiness/john-locke/.

Tocqueville, Alexis de. *Democracy in America: A New Translation by George Lawrence.* New York: Harper & Row, 1966.

"Alexis de Tocqueville." Wikipedia. Last edited March 14, 2022. https://en.wikipedia.org/wiki/Alexis_de_Tocqueville.

THANK YOU

This book would not have been possible without the encouragement, support, and contributions from my remarkable wife, Mary. She helped develop the overall concept and gave invaluable input on the six principles, stories, and chapters. Other family members also provided helpful insights: Jay Glauser, Aunalisa Arellano, Tyler Glauser, and Jaime Glauser. In addition, friends, scholars, and content experts provided feedback on various chapters and the entire manuscript: Dr. Camille Fronk Olson, Dr. Ron Larkin, Bruce Jensen, Andrea Diamond, Lisa Adams, Anna Lisa Davidson, Wendy Keller, Natalee Champlin, Cass McNally, Becky Burbidge, Andrea Moesser, and Elizabeth Moesser McMillan. And a special thanks to my good friend Willus Branham, who designed the clever icons and interior graphics in the book.

The team at Lioncrest Publishing has also been amazing. Paul Fair provided a valuable concept review, Skyler Gray helped create the title, and the gifted Anna Dorfman designed the perfect cover. In addition, three talented editors helped clean up the manuscript: Marie Kuipers, Joyce Li, and Gillian Glover. And finally, Mikey

Kershisnik has been a superb project manager who brought all the pieces together to create the book I have dreamed about for many years.

Made in the USA
Las Vegas, NV
17 December 2022

63015493R00146